THE CRISIS OF THE DEEPER LIFE

The Crisis
of the
Deeper Life

Dr. George P. Pardington

Christian Publications

CAMP HILL, PENNSYLVANIA

Christian Publications
3825 Hartzdale Drive, Camp Hill, PA 17011

The mark of ◖✝◗ vibrant faith

ISBN: 0-87509-454-6
LOC Catalog Card Number: 91-70910
© 1991 by Christian Publications
All rights reserved
Printed in the United States of America

91 92 93 94 95   5 4 3 2 1

Cover photo credit: Comstock

CONTENTS

INTRODUCTION

The *Crisis of the Deeper Life* is an integral part of the life and history of The Christian and Missionary Alliance. Many generations of Alliance missionaries and ministers have found their way to the fullness of the Holy Spirit through the writings of George Pardington. For over 50 years this book was required reading for every ordinand serving in the Alliance. Although Pardington's exegesis is sometimes debatable, the theme and heartbeat of the book remain as relevant today as ever.

While we all agree that at the time of regeneration we are born of the Spirit, there is, however, a crisis of the deeper life when the Holy Spirit fills and controls our whole person.

To insist that Pardington embrace the popularly approved terminology of today is to lay aside a volume that God has used to lead scores of people to the crisis of the deeper life. In this edition we have chosen to allow Pardington to be Pardington. This means his terminology as well as his message. This truth is so basic to Christian living we must issue this volume once again. It may well be that, as Martin Lloyd-Jones has intimated, evangelicals will ultimately return to older terminology.

Whatever the future may hold, this present volume is sent forth with the earnest prayer that you will read its message with an open mind and a receptive heart. May God bring renewal of this truth to a Church that desperately needs revival.

Richard W. Bailey
Vice President/Division of Church Ministries
The Christian and Missionary Alliance

CHAPTER

1

All in Christ

"Christianity is not character, but Christ." This utterance by Woodrow Wilson, while president of Princeton University, expresses both the simplest fact and the profoundest philosophy of the gospel. Christianity presents a sharp contrast to all other religions.

For an example, compare Buddhism and Islam. Like Christianity they are missionary religions. But as religious systems, they exist entirely apart from their founders. It is true that Buddha and Mohammed are worshiped by their respective devotees, but they have only a historic relationship to the religions which they founded. In no way is Buddhism dependent upon Buddha, nor Islam upon Mohammed. With Christianity, however, exactly the opposite is true. Jesus Christ appeared in history, founded a religion, and is worshiped by His followers.

Thus far Christianity is like Buddhism and Islam, but at this point the resemblance ceases. For while Buddha and Mohammed died, Jesus Christ lives.

Moreover, Christianity is not like other religions, merely a body of teaching, nor a round of ceremonies, nor is it even a code of ethics. It has, indeed, a body of teaching, which is the sum of revealed truth; it has ceremonial rites, which are divine ordinances; and it has a system of ethics, which is the highest in the world. But Christianity is more than doctrine, more than ordinances, more even than morality. In fact, as the term is commonly employed, Christianity is not a religion. It is a life. Its essential element is the vital union of the soul with God. Apart from the person of the Lord Jesus Christ, not merely as the historic Founder, but as the supreme Fountain of a new life of divine knowledge, love and power, Christianity would exist only in name. Take Christ from Christianity, and it would descend to the level of one of the religions of the world. Jesus Christ is the sum of all doctrine, the source of all virtue and the spring of all service. Hence, it is true that Christianity is Christ and Christ is Christianity.

Writing on this very point, in his little handbook on the *Evidences of Christianity*, Canon Row, of England, says:

> Christianity differs from every other known religion in the fact that it is based on the person of its Founder. He is the sole foundation on which the church rests; the principle of its unity; the inspiring motive to holiness; the spiritual power which makes the Christian strong in the discharge of every duty; in a word, Jesus Christ may be said to constitute Christianity itself. In

proof of this, I say, read your New Testaments and you will see that what I say is true. The Revised Version (my edition) consists of one hundred and ninety-four pages, and there are not five in which the sacred name does not occur, or is not directly alluded to, and in some it occurs 20 times. Of all the religions now existing in the world, Buddhism is said to number 400 million, and Mohammedanism, over 120 million votaries; yet if we were to strike the person of Sakya Mundi, the founder of Buddhism, and that of Mohammed, of Mohammedanism, out of their respective systems, their religions, as systems of religion, would remain intact. The same is true of Brahmanism, Confucianism, Zoroastrianism, and every other religion of the past or present. It is true even of Judaism, for the person of Moses might be removed out of it, but the system would remain intact. All these religions have had founders, but they have not one of them erected their systems on their own persons. But Christianity is so based on the person of its Founder that if we remove every reference to Jesus Christ out of the New Testament, the brief remainder becomes a mass of shapeless ruins.

As a life, Christianity may be defined as the union of the soul with Christ. This sublime truth finds symbolic representation and explicit statement in the New Testament.

There are five symbolic representations of this vital relationship:

I. The Architectural figure, or the relation existing between the foundation and the building.

> Built on the foundation of the apostles and prophets, with Christ Jesus himself as the chief cornerstone. In him the whole building is joined together and rises to become a holy temple in the Lord. And in him you too are being built together to become a dwelling in which God lives by his Spirit. (Ephesians 2:20–22)

> Rooted and built up in him, strengthened in the faith as you were taught, and overflowing with thankfulness. (Colossians 1:23)

> As you come to him, the living Stone—rejected by men but chosen by God and precious to him—you also, like living stones, are being built into a spiritual house to be a holy priesthood, offering spiritual sacrifices acceptable to God through Jesus Christ. (1 Peter 2:4–5)

With these passages the reader may also compare Psalm 118:22 and Isaiah 28:16.

Jesus Christ is the foundation and His people are the building. The key which interprets the spiritual meaning of this symbol is the Inhabitation, or Indwelling. The occupant of the temple of believers is the Holy Spirit.

"What agreement is there between the temple of God and idols? For we are the temple of the living God. As God has said: 'I will live with them and walk among them, and I will be their God, and they will be my people' " (2 Corinthians 6:16).

II. The Marital figure or the relation existing between husband and wife.

> So, my brothers, you also died to the law through the body of Christ, that you might belong to another, to him who was raised from the dead, in order that we might bear fruit to God. (Romans 7:4)

> I am jealous for you with a godly jealousy. I promised you to one husband, to Christ, so that I might present you as a pure virgin to him. (2 Corinthians 11:2)

> "For this reason a man will leave his father and mother and be united to his wife, and the two will become one flesh." This is a profound mystery—but I am talking about Christ and the church. (Ephesians 5:31–32)

> Let us rejoice and be glad/ and give him glory!/ For the wedding of the Lamb has come,/ and his bride has made herself ready. (Revelation 19:7)

> The Spirit and the bride say, "Come!" And let him who hears say, "Come!" Whoever is thirsty,

let him come; and whoever wishes, let him take the free gift of the water of life. (Revelation 22:17)

Christ is the Husband and His people constitute His bride, the love. The Old Testament abounds in allusions to this relationship between Jehovah and Israel. Read, for example, Song of Songs, and see also Hosea 2:14–23. The result of this holy relationship between Christ and the believer is the fruit of the Spirit (Galatians 5:22–23).

III. The Vegetable figure or the relation existing between the vine and the branches.

The beautiful allegory of the divine and the branches in John 15:1–16, is an unfolding of this vital union between Christ and the believer. It should be very carefully studied. Read also Romans 11:17–24.

If we have been united with him like this in his death, we will certainly also be united with him in his resurrection. (Romans 6:5)

So then, just as you received Christ Jesus as Lord, continue to live in him, rooted and built up in him, strengthened in the faith as you were taught, and overflowing with thankfulness. (Colossians 2:6–7)

Christ is the true Vine, and His people are the spiritual branches. The key which interprets the spiritual meaning of this symbol is fruitfulness. Read Psalm 80 and Isaiah 27:2–3.

IV. The Physical figure, or the relation existing between the Head and the body.

Do you not know that your bodies are members of Christ himself? Shall I then take the members of Christ and unite them with a prostitute? Never! Do you not know that your body is a temple of the Holy Spirit, who is in you, whom you have received from God? You are not your own. (1 Corinthians 6:15,19)

The body is a unit, though it is made up of many parts; and though all its parts are many, they form one body. So it is with Christ. Now you are the body of Christ, and each one of you is a part of it. (1 Corinthians 12:12, 27) The whole passage—verses 12–27—will prove valuable if carefully studied.

And God placed all things under his feet and appointed him to be head over everything for the church, which is his body, the fullness of him who fills everything in every way. (Ephesians 1:22–23)

Instead, speaking the truth in love, we will in all things grow up into him who is the Head, that is, Christ. (Ephesians 4:15)

> After all, no one ever hated his own body, but he feeds and cares for it, just as Christ does the church—for we are members of his body. (Ephesians 5:29–30).

Christ is the Head, and the Church is the body. The key which interprets the spiritual meaning of this symbol is completeness and mutual dependence and administration. In First Corinthians 12:12, there is a striking expression: the Church is called Christ.

V. The Racial figure, or the relation existing between Adam and Christ.

In the fifth chapter of Romans, verses 12–21, a historic and doctrinal parallel is drawn by the apostle Paul between Adam and Christ. To understand this passage is to be well grounded in the doctrines of sin and grace.

> For as in Adam all die, so in Christ all will be made alive. So it is written: "The first man Adam became a living being," the last Adam, a life-giving spirit. And just as we have borne the likeness of the earthly man, so shall we bear the likeness of the man from heaven. (1 Corinthians 15:22, 45, 49)

Adam is the head of the natural race, and Christ is the Head of the spiritual race. The key which interprets the spiritual meaning of this symbol is representation, or what is called in theological language, "federal headship."

Then there are in the New Testament a number of explicit statements of this vital union between Christ and the believer. For example, believers are said to be in Christ and Christ is said to be in believers.

> On that day you will realize that I am in my Father, and you are in me, and I am in you. (John 14:20)

> Remain in me, and I will remain in you. No branch can bear fruit by itself; it must remain in the vine. Neither can you bear fruit unless you remain in me. (John 15:4)

Again, both the Father and the Son are said to be in the believer. "Jesus replied, 'If anyone loves me, he will obey my teaching. My Father will love him, and we will come to him and make our home with him' " (John 14:23).

Christian experience, in its varied phases, may be expressed in terms of the believer's union with Christ. For example, conversion is the sinner's turning to God in repentance and faith to be united to Christ. Justification is the new standing that the believer has through union with Christ. Regeneration is the new life that is imparted to the believer through union with Christ. And Sanctification is the purity and maturity of the believer's life through union with Christ.

Essential characteristics

Some essential characteristics of the believer's union with Christ may be mentioned:

First, it is *organic.* In Ephesians 5:30 we read: "for we are members of his body."

Second, it is *vital.* In Galatians 2:20 we read: "I have been crucified with Christ and I no longer live, but Christ lives in me. The life I live in the body, I live by faith in the Son of God, who loved me and gave himself for me."

Third, it is *spiritual.* In First Corinthians 6:17 we read: "But he who unites himself with the Lord is one with him in spirit."

Fourth, it is *mysterious.* In Colossians 1:27 we read: "To them God has chosen to make known among the Gentiles the glorious riches of this mystery, which is Christ in you, the hope of glory."

Fifth, it is *eternal.* In John 10:28 we read: "I give them eternal life, and they shall never perish; no one can snatch them out of my hand."

This supreme fact of the essential connection between Christ and Christianity, on the one hand, finds expression in the simple watchword of The Christian and Missionary Alliance: "Christ our Savior, Sanctifier, Healer and Coming King." This familiar phrase is popularly called "The Fourfold Gospel." The Alliance has neither a so-called formal creed nor official confession of faith. It has not felt the need of one. For it is in substantial accord with evangelical truth, and in common with the various denominations accepts the great body of Protestant theology. By this we mean such fundamental doctrines as: the verbal inspiration of the Holy Scriptures as originally given, the Deity and vicarious atonement of the Lord Jesus Christ, the lost condition of the sinner, the necessity of the new birth, the personality and deeper life of the Holy Ghost, the evangelization of the world, the second coming of the Lord, the eternal salvation of those who believe in Christ and the everlasting punishment of those who reject Him.

But the Alliance has a special calling and a distinctive testimony. This finds expression in the simple and popular statement of "The Calling and Work of the Alliance."

> Pre-eminently we are witnesses to Christ. We are glad to testify to Him before we speak of any of His blessing or gifts to men. It is Christ as a Person, as a living reality, as the supreme fact of history and life, Jesus Himself, Who is the theme of our testimony. Soon He is to appear in the vivid and glorious revelation of His personal majesty, filling all earth and heaven. But meanwhile He is projecting His personality upon the age, upon the thought and heart of His people, and upon our individual lives, and He wants us to know Him, to represent Him and to reveal Him to men. Above everything else this is a Christ movement. If we are saved it is Christ Who saves us. If we are sanctified it is Christ Who is made unto us sanctification. If we are healed it is because His life is in us. And the hope of the future is not

the glory He is to reveal, but the return of our King Himself, our Beloved and our Friend.

To give salvation to the sinner, to make Christ real to the believer, to present Christ in His fullness through the power of the indwelling Holy Ghost as the complete satisfaction of every need of spirit, mind and body, to give Christ and the riches of His grace to the heathen world: this is our special calling and distinctive testimony. In a word, the mission and message of The Christian and Missionary Alliance is to proclaim neglected Scripture truth and to prosecute neglected Christian work both at home and abroad: "to give the whole gospel to the whole world."

Preach Christ

From the beginning it has been the spirit of our movement not so much to preach doctrine as to preach Christ. The aim has been to avoid the controversial side of disputed questions, and to present "the fullness of Jesus" for Christian life and service. Take, for example, the second part of our attractive watchword: "Christ our Sanctifier." This phrase expresses at once the simplest fact and the profoundest philosophy of holiness. On this supremely important theme it is our mission and our message to present the living Lord, who is "made unto us sanctification." So far as possible we leave the plane of theory and rise to the simple and sublime truth of the indwelling Christ. We do not, therefore, emphasize inner states and subjective experiences as much as we emphasize the Lord.

We do not magnify the blessing; we magnify the Blesser. We do not talk about "it" but about "Him."

A story is told of a London clergyman who visited a woman troubled about her soul. She could not understand the way of faith. The minister noticed that she was in destitute circumstances. Giving her sixpence, he asked her what she could get with it.

"Why sir," replied the woman, "I can get a pennyworth of bread, a pennyworth of coals, a ha'pennyworth of sugar, a ha'pennyworth of wood, a ha'penny candle,—and then I shall have a ha'penny left."

"But how," inquired the clergyman, "can you get so much for so little?"

"You see, sir," responded the woman, "it's all in the sixpence."

"Well, but how," he asked, "did you get the sixpence?"

"Why, sir," she said, "you gave it to me, and I took it."

Then the minister said: "My good woman, God is offering you Jesus Christ, just as I offered you the sixpence. Will you not take His gift just as you took my sixpence? If you will accept Christ, you will find that just as the food, the warmth, and the light are 'all in the sixpence,' so all you need is in Him."

But while emphasizing the indwelling Christ, the Alliance has always clearly and unmistakably stood for "a real genuine experience of righteousness of heart and life." In the language of one of our official leaflets this means:

. . . a testimony of a life of holiness, a mighty complete inworking of the grace and power of God, sufficient to overcome the power of sin, to lift us above the dominance of self, to fill us with the Spirit of God, and to reproduce in us the very life of Christ Himself.

It (this testimony) meets the hunger of a great multitude of weary, dissatisfied and defeated lives, who are asking, "Is there not something better than this life of sin and failure? Is there not as much power in our Christ to keep us now as there will be some day to glorify us in heaven beyond?" And we tell them that "He is able to save unto the uttermost all that come unto God by Him." But we are not too fastidious about phases and phrases if there is real genuine experience of righteousness of heart and life; but we love to emphasize the Christ side of holiness; not self perfection, not the restoration of what Adam lost, but a divine life-union with God, the nature of Jesus Himself, the indwelling and overcoming power of the Holy Spirit; not as the result of a slow and toilsome struggle, but as the free gift of grace bestowed upon every surrendered and believing heart.

Renewed character and righteous conduct

Sanctification is not a garment to conceal unrighteousness. It is not a veneering to hide a life spiritually untransformed. Sanctification means renewed character and righteous conduct. It involves a radical revolution in personality. There is a change in the temper of the mind, in the disposition of the heart and in the bent of the will. But the blessing of a clean heart is inseparable from the possession of the clean heart by the Holy Ghost. Without His presence the cleansing of the temple would not be permanent. Sanctification is not ours apart from the person of Christ. We are holy only as we are in vital union with the Holy One. When we get *Him*, we get *everything* in Him. Romans 8:32 says,

> He who did not spare his own Son, but gave him up for us all—how will he not also, along with him, graciously give us all things?

Thus our watchword for a holy life and a fruitful ministry is: "Everything in Jesus, and Jesus everything."

Newness of Life

There is a progress of divine truth and of Christian experience. All God's works, whether in creation or redemption, have a beginning, a development, and a completion. Of the spiritual world, as well as of the natural world, the law is: "All by itself the soil produces grain—first the stalk, then the head, then the full kernel in the head" (Mark 4:28).

Holiness is not the first step in Christian experience. The new birth is the starting point. Before we can know Christ as our Sanctifier, we must know Him as our Savior. Before spiritual life can be deepened, it must be received.

There is no fact more clearly revealed in the Scriptures than that man is a wanderer from God. Like the prodigal son he has left his God. Like the prodigal son he has left his Father's house. This is the first scene in the drama of redemption: the race of Adam is *lost*. Man is a sinner—a rebel against God, and as the result of sin his mind is darkened, his heart degraded and his will depraved.

The Lord saw how great man's wickedness on the earth had become, and that every inclination of the thoughts of his heart was only evil all the time. (Genesis 6:5)

Who can bring what is pure from the impure? No one! (Job 14:4)

What is man, that he could be pure, or one born of woman, that he could be righteous? (Job 15:14)

Surely I was sinful at birth,/ sinful from the time my mother conceived me. (Psalm 51:5)

Even from birth the wicked go astray;/ from the womb they are wayward and speak lies. (Psalm 58:3)

There is not a righteous man on earth who does what is right and never sins. (Ecclesiastes 7:20)

For out of the heart come evil thoughts, murder, adultery, sexual immorality, theft, false testimony, slander. (Matthew 15:19)

As it is written: "There is no one righteous, not even one; there is no one who understands, no one who seeks God. All have turned away, they have together become worthless; there is no one who does good, not even one." (Romans 3:10–12)

For all have sinned and fall short of the glory of God. (Romans 3:23)

Therefore, just as sin entered the world through one man, and death through sin, and in this way death came to all men, because all sinned. (Romans 5:12)

All of us also lived among them at one time, gratifying the cravings of our sinful nature and following its desires and thoughts. (Ephesians 2:3)

They are darkened in their understanding and separated from the life of God because of the ignorance that is in them due to the hardening of their hearts. (Ephesians 4:18)

But, saddest of all, the world does not know its doom. Sinners are blinded to their lost estate. Like the wretched prodigal, they are in a "far country," wasting their substance "with riotous living." They have no sense of impending peril and are giving themselves up to the engrossing pressure of business or the pursuit of pleasure.

The sinner is like a little girl, who was found crying on the street of a great city.

"My child," said a kind-hearted policeman, who found her, "you are lost. Come with me."

"No," replied the little one, "I am not lost. I am all right; but *my mamma is lost.*"

Sinners are lost

So today sinners are wondering where God is: some are doubting His existence; others are questioning His love and providential care. Yet men and women are lost, and Jesus Christ "came to seek and save what was lost" (Luke 10:10b). In the ear of every poor sinner rings the question that God asked His first wandering child, "Adam, where are you?" Sinner you are lost, *lost!* LOST!! Do you realize that you are? "Remember that at that time you were separate from Christ, excluded from citizenship in Israel and foreigners to the covenants of the promise, without hope and without God in the world" (Ephesians 2:12).

The next scene in the working out of redemption is the Father's love. Man forsook God; God did not forsake man. The father in the parable of the prodigal son represents God. It grieved the father to have his boy leave home, and go out alone in the world. Yet he did not forcibly detain his son. Contrary to this father's wishes, the young man made his choice, and had to abide by the consequences, disastrous as they were. Although grief filled his heart, the father did not stop loving his son. He did more: he saw to it that on his own part there was no obstacle in the way of the wanderer's return at any time. He kept the latchstring out and a light always burning in the window. Every morning and evening he climbed the hilltop in front of the house, and shading his eyes with his hands looked eagerly and anxiously for any sign of his wandering boy's return.

This is a picture of the heart of God. Although man disobeyed God, yet God did not cease to love him. He grieved over his rebellion and yearned for his return. But God went farther than the father in the parable. He took active measures toward the sinner's return. His heart prompted, His wisdom devised and His power provided a way of redemption. This brings us to the third picture of salvation—the cross. We are apt to get the matter wrong. We think that God loves us, because Christ died for us. Whereas it is just the other way: Christ died for us, because God loves us. Listen!

> For God so loved the world that he gave his one and only Son, that whoever believes in him shall not perish but have eternal life. (John 3:16)

> But God demonstrates his own love for us in this: While we were still sinners, Christ died for us. (Romans 5:8)

The cross of Christ tells the story of the love of God for a lost race. Christ died for sinners. This is the heart of the gospel. The innocent Son of God took the place of the guilty son of Adam. Christ took the place of the sinner in judgment and Himself bore the penalty of his sin. This is the meaning of the blood.

Sinner, have you had a vision of the cross? Do you realize that Christ died for you and on the "cruel tree" bore your sins? More than this: do you see that in the person of your substitute, if you accept Jesus Christ as your Substitute, you have been executed, and that now the law of God has no claim against you? Do you know that by His death the Lord Jesus has reconciled you to God? Do you know that by simple faith the Savior may be yours, and that you may have peace with God? Only sin can blind you to these glorious truths. Oh, look to Jesus and live! "There is life for a look at the Crucified One."

The next picture in the pilgrim's progress is the wanderer's decision to return to his Father's house. It was while he was tending swine and feeding on husks that the prodigal "came to his senses," remembered the abundance of his father's house, and resolved to go back. He exclaimed: "I will set out and go back to my father and say to him: Father, I have sinned against heaven and against you. I am no longer worthy to be called your son; make me like one of your hired men (Luke 15:18–19).

Spiritually, this means that at last the eyes of the sinner are open. He sees his lost condition, and he decides to return to Christ. Two steps will bring the sinner to the Savior. One is repentance, and the other is faith. The result of taking these two steps is conversion. Strictly speaking, conversion is a human process rather than a divine work. The word means, literally, "a turning around." The sinner performs the military evolution of "right about face." Instead of facing the world he now faces God.

First step is repentance

The first step in conversion is repentance. The Greek word, *metanoia*, signifies, literally, "a change of mind." Thus Jesus said, "The time has come. The kingdom of God is near. Repent and believe the good news!" (Mark 1:15).

There are three things in repentance. First, a recognition of sin. This is an intellectual process. Second, a godly sorrow for sin. This is an emotional element. It is deep, sincere contrition of heart. Yet of itself it does not save. There is needed the third factor: a forsaking of sin. This is a decision of the will. It is the actual turning away from sin. Sam Jones expresses it: "Quit your meanness." Repentance is the fruit of conviction of sin. No one can produce conviction of sin in his own heart. It is the work of the Holy Spirit.

> When he comes, he will convict the world of guilt in regard to sin and righteousness and judgment. (John 16:8)

Faith is turning toward God

Just as repentance is a turning from sin, so faith is a turning toward God. In nature, faith is in part *certainty*, and in part *trust*. In one aspect it is a kind of sixth sense—a spiritual sense, taking the place of evidence in material things. "Now faith is being sure of what we hope for and certain of what we do not see" (Hebrews 11:1).

It is commonly said "Seeing is believing." But in reality the opposite of this is the truth: "Believing is seeing." That is, believing is spiritual sight. One who believes requires no other proof. *His faith is his proof.*

But in another aspect faith is trust, a reliance of the soul upon God.

> Commit your way to the Lord; trust in him and he will do this. (Psalm 37:5)

As to its source, faith is both human and divine. By the mysterious and gracious working of the Holy Spirit the sinner can believe upon Christ for salvation, and God requires him to do it. Thus, the Philippian jailer inquired of Paul and Silas:

> "Sirs, what must I do to be saved?" They replied, "Believe in the Lord Jesus and you will be saved—you and your household." (Acts 16:30–31)

In the decision of his will to believe, God meets the sinner with the gracious power to believe. Thus faith is the gift of God and the fruit of the Spirit.

> For it is by grace you have been saved, through faith—and this not from yourselves, it is the gift of God. (Ephesians 2:8)

> But the fruit of the Spirit is . . . faith. (Galatians 5:22)

There is a point, however, where our faith breaks down and we have to receive the faith of God. Yea, more; we must take Christ to believe in us. Paul exclaimed, "I have been crucified with Christ and I no longer live, but Christ lives in me. The life I live in the body, I live by faith in the Son of God, who loved me and gave himself for me" (Galatians 2:20). The King James Version puts the phrase this way: "I live by the faith of the Son of God."

Now, conversion must be sound and thorough. Along with repentance must go, when necessary, reparation and restitution. Reparation means the repairing of an injury. For example, if anything unkind or unjust has been said or done, it must be rectified by confession and reconciliation. Restitution means the restoring of that which does not belong to one. For example, if before conversion, a fraud has been practiced or a theft committed, the matter must be made right by confession and restoration. Confession alone is not sufficient. The stolen goods must be returned or if that is impossible, the just equivalent must be given. In similar circumstances Zaccheus restored fourfold. "Look, Lord! Here and now I give half of my possessions to the poor, and if I have cheated anybody out of anything, I will pay back four times the amount" (Luke 19:8).

Reconciliation and restoration

The final picture of the sinner's return is one of reconciliation and restoration. The prodigal son "got up and went to his father" (Luke 15:20). And when he reached his father's house he found a welcome in his father's heart. The old man ran to meet the returning wanderer, and fell on his neck and kissed him. The boy had a set speech ready, but he either forgot the latter part or was not permitted to finish it. The father had the best robe put upon his son, a ring placed on his hand and shoes on his feet. The fatted calf was killed and the whole household began to eat and be merry. The father's heart was bursting with joy, as he exclaimed: " 'For this son of mine was dead and is alive again; he was lost and is found.' So they began to celebrate" (Luke 15:24).

Sinner, may you like the prodigal son, not only come to yourself, but also get up and go to your Father. God has come far more than half way. One step, and one step only, will bring you to His heart. This is the choice of your will. God pleads with you, but will not coerce you. "Turn! Turn from your evil ways! Why will you die" (Ezekiel 33:11b). Sinner, backslider, this is the hour of mercy. Take Christ as your Savior. Backslider, return now unto your Father's house! Then God will clothe you with the garment of salvation—the robe of Christ's righteousness. He will give you the kiss of reconciliation, put on your hand the ring of restored fellowship, clad your feet with the preparation of the gospel of peace and there will be joy in heaven among the angels over the sinner that repents and over the backslider that returns to his Father's house.

This transformation of a sinner into a believer is known in doctrinal language as justification and regeneration. These terms may be separated in thought but not in experience. At the same time that God justifies He also regenerates. Let us look a little at these two things.

Justification

First, *justification*. The sinner is a law breaker and under sentence of punishment. In the act of justification God pardons him. But He does more than that. He treats the sinner as if he had never done wrong. In the Scriptures to *justify* means not to *make*, but to *declare* righteous. It is a term taken from the usages of law, and describes a change in the *standing* of a person and not in his *character*. When justified, the sinner stands before the law of God, not merely as a guilty man who has been pardoned, but as an innocent man who never has done wrong. Understand clearly, it is not that the sinner is not guilty and deserving of punishment, but rather that because of Christ's death in his stead and because of his faith in Christ as his substitute *the sinner is treated as if he were innocent*.

Thus, justification is obtained in a two-fold way. First, by the blood of Christ, and second, by the faith of the sinner.

> [All] are justified freely by his grace through the redemption that came by Jesus Christ. (Romans 3:24)

> Therefore, since we have been justified through faith, we have peace with God through our Lord Jesus Christ. (Romans 5:1)

Of course the blood of Christ means not only His death but His resurrection as well.

He was delivered over to death for our sins and was raised to life for our justification. (Romans 4:25)

Regeneration

Second, *regeneration.* But now, what is regeneration? We have said that at the time God justifies He also regenerates. Well, *justification* changes the sinner's *standing,* but regeneration changes his *character.* Justification gives a new relationship to God, but regeneration gives a new life in God. In other words, justification is the legal transformation of a sinner into a believer, while regeneration is the actual transformation. Let us notice a few of them.

I. A new heart and a new spirit.

I will give you a new heart and put a new spirit in you; I will remove from you your heart of stone and give you a heart of flesh. (Ezekiel 36:26)

Now, we must recognize that this verse is part of a passage that refers primarily to Israel, and is yet to be literally fulfilled in the future. But at the same time this section, chapter 36:25–38, has a deeply spiritual significance. This verse may properly be taken as a promise of new life in Christ. The reader will notice that the thought of substitution is presented: the old is set aside, and the new is imparted. For the "heart of stone" a "heart of flesh" or a "new heart" is given, and a "new spirit" is implanted.

II. Born again, or born "from above."

> In reply Jesus declared, "I tell you the truth, no one can see the kingdom of God unless he is born again." (John 3:3)

Our Lord's conversation with Nicodemus in the third chapter of John may be regarded as a succession of contrasts. There is first, the contrast between natural birth and spiritual birth (verses 3–5). Then there is second, the contrast between the flesh and the spirit. "Flesh gives birth to flesh, but the Spirit gives birth to spirit" (John 3:6). And then there is third, the contrast between "earthly things" and "heavenly things." (verse 12). Now the main point in this connection is that the new life in God, here described as "born again" and "born of the Spirit" is not earth, nor of the flesh. It is "from above" and "of the Spirit."

> . . . children born not of natural descent, nor of human decision or a husband's will, but born of God. (John 1:13)

III. A passing from death unto life.

> I tell you the truth, whoever hears my word and believes in him who sent me has eternal life and

will not be condemned; he has crossed over from death to life. (John 5:24)

Death is not only the separation of the soul from the body but also the separation of the soul from God. To be cut off from contact with God is death—moral death. Death is one of the terms used in the Scriptures to describe the condition of the sinner. And the imparting of spiritual life is described as a quickening from death.

But because of his great love for us, God, who is rich in mercy, made us alive with Christ even when we were dead in transgressions—it is by grace you have been saved. And God raised us up with Christ and seated us with him in the heavenly realms in Christ Jesus. (Ephesians 2:4–6)

IV. A new creation.

Therefore, if anyone is in Christ, he is a new creation; the old has gone, the new has come! (2 Corinthians 5:17)

Neither circumcision nor uncircumcision means anything; what counts is a new creation. (Galatians 6:15)

Here a radical distinction is made between natural life and spiritual life, between the old creation and the new creation. In Romans 6:4, we read that we are to walk "in new life." In the New Testament there are two Greek adjectives translated "new." One is *neos*, denoting what is new in time, and the other is *kainos*, signifying what is new in nature. The word "new" in the phrase "new life" is a noun formed from the latter adjective, and denotes a new kind or quality of life. The only other occurrence of this Greek noun in the New Testament is in Romans 7:6—"in the new way of the Spirit, and not in the old way of the written code"—where the meaning is the same, viz., the new kind of life which we receive from the Holy Spirit.

> He who was seated on the throne said, "I am making everything new!" (Revelation 21:5)

V. A partaking of the Divine nature.

> Through these he has given us his very great and precious promises, so that through them you may participate in the divine nature and escape the corruption in the world caused by evil desires. (2 Peter 1:4)

This is perhaps the nearest approach to a definition of any of the descriptions of regeneration that we have examined. Almost exclusively in the words of Scripture we may say, "to be born from above is to become a participant in the divine nature." Dr. A.J. Gordon says: "Regeneration is the communication of the divine nature to man by the operation of the Holy Spirit through the Word." In the new birth there is both an operation of the Spirit of God and an agency of the Word of God.

> Jesus answered, "I tell you the truth, no one can enter the kingdom of God unless he is born of water and the Spirit." (John 3:5)

> For you have been born again, not of perishable seed, but of imperishable, through the living and enduring word of God. (1 Peter 1:23).

Mysterious in all its varied forms is the nature of life. All we know is something of its characteristics. We know, for example, that there are different grades of life, each grade separate and distinct from all the others. Thus, a product of the vegetable kingdom can never become a product of the animal kingdom. Between the two kingdoms there is an impassable gulf. Again, an animal can never develop into a man. To borrow a figure, your pet dog can never be as one of the children. It has the nature and mind of a dog, and no amount of petting or training can make it anything else but a dog. It cannot enter intelligently into the sympathies and interests of the family circle. In like manner, a sinner cannot grow into a Christian. The mightiest philosopher that ever lived can never by natural process become a child of God. Jesus said: "Flesh gives birth to flesh, but Spirit gives birth to spirit" (John 3:6).

An amiable disposition, a gentle spirit, a courteous manner, personal charm, and sterling worth—all these things are desirable and perhaps essential qualities of moral character, but of themselves they do not furnish evidence of the possession of spiritual life. The new birth is not education, nor culture, nor character. It is life, a new life, eternal life, the very life of God in the soul of man. As someone has said, "The Christian life is a Christ-life."

In the Wilderness

It is a great thing to be saved. But salvation is only the letter A of the alphabet of Christian experience. In emphasizing the importance of sanctification it is unnecessary to minimize the equal importance of regeneration. It is to be feared that some people are striving to understand the deeper truths of the gospel who have never received spiritual life.

There is joy in heaven and on earth when a soul is born into the kingdom of God. The heart of the new convert overflows with peace and gladness, and his lips are filled with praises to God. The language of his soul is:

> He brought me out of the miry clay,
> He put my feet on the rock to stay;
> He puts a song in my heart today,
> A song of praise, Hallelujah!

It is a good thing for the children of God to recall

the time of their first love. You remember, beloved, how it all was. You lived in a new world. The divine light and heavenly glory in your soul were reflected upon your surroundings. Everything looked different. Even the most familiar things were not quite the same. There was a new light upon sea and sky. The birds sang more sweetly. The grass was greener. All nature in its varied forms spoke to you in voices which before you could not understand.

> Everywhere, everywhere,
> In the earth, and sea, and air,
> God, His wond'rous works declare,
> God is present everywhere.

You were never so happy before in all your life. Cares and responsibilities sat lightly upon you. You seemed to be walking on air. Life wore on like a beautiful dream, full of heavenly romance, and you often found yourself wondering if it could all be real. It seemed almost too good to be true. Of course such manifestations of spiritual exaltation are rarely present in every instance in their full intensity, for the temperament and training of Christians modify and color their religious experience.

A subtle change

After a little, however, a change came. It was not, perhaps, that the heavenly light in the soul faded, nor that the divine glory grew dim, nor yet that the song of praise died out on the lips. But somehow things were not the same. Temptations came that were not overcome. You found that you did not have the mastery over sin. The first fall took you by surprise. You were not prepared for it. You were cast down, and waves of disappointment broke over your soul. But you took the matter to your Savior. In grief and penitence you told Him all about it. Easily and quickly you found forgiveness and restoration, and then went on your way rejoicing with renewed confidence. But soon the experience was repeated. You wondered what it all meant.

Though tempted to do so, you could not doubt your conversion. But you became discouraged. You found your experience uneven and your path crooked. One day you were on the mountain singing, the next you were in the valley sighing. Yet you had the sense of the Savior's presence. Your heart was often warmed by His love. Indeed, His love seemed never more tender than when you came to Him in defeat. Moreover, you had answers to prayer. You were, however, conscious of much weakness and many failures in your life.

As you prayerfully studied the Bible and learned that God is holy and that He hates sin and requires His children to be free from it, your heart gladly responded, and you longed to be pure. But somehow you found that you could not overcome the evil in your life. You discovered the presence of something within that resisted God, rebelled against His law, and continually brought you into the bondage of defeat. You began to struggle against this inner enemy of your soul. You promised the Lord that you would not sin, but you could not keep your promise. Will power was exerted but did not avail. Resolutions were made but broken as often as made. The *love* of sin was gone, but its *power* was not destroyed.

A place of blessing

Such an experience as this comes to every child of God. It corresponds spiritually to the wilderness wanderings of the children of Israel. In Christian typology Egypt represents the world; the crossing of the Red Sea represents separations from the world, or conversion; the passage of the Jordan represents the death of self; and the land of Canaan represents sanctification, or the rest of faith that remains for the people of God. But between the Red Sea and River Jordan was the Wilderness of Sinai, in which for nearly 40 years the Israelites wandered.

This desert life was characterized by a "mixed multitude" and a mixed experience. On the one hand, there were many manifestations of divine favor and blessing. The pillar of cloud and fire led the people in the way, and delivered them from their enemies (Exodus 13:21–22). There were the sweetened waters of Marah, with the statute and promise of physical healing (Exodus 15:23–26). There were the 12 wells of Elim and the 70 palm trees, speaking of refreshment and spiritual rest (Exodus 15:27). Then there was the manna that fell every morning and fed the people throughout their journey (Exodus 16:1–5, 14–25). And then there was the smitten rock that followed them and satisfied their thirst (Exodus 17:1–7). Surely, the wilderness was a place of divine presence, divine preservation, divine promise and divine performance. God entered the desert with His people, went with them through all their pilgrimage, and abundantly blessed them.

A place of testing

But on the other hand, the wilderness was a place of testing and trial, ending in defeat and disaster. The Israelites murmured against Moses and Aaron (Exodus 16:3). They longed for the cucumbers, the melons, the leeks and onions and the garlic of Egypt (Numbers 11:5). Their souls loathed the light manna, and they lusted for flesh. Because of this they were bitten by the fiery serpents (Numbers 21:1–9). Moreover, the people often disobeyed the Lord. And finally, at Kadesh Barnea, they openly rebelled against Him by refusing at His command to enter the land of promise. They lost their inheritance through unbelief:

> And with whom was he angry for forty years? Was it not with those who sinned, whose bodies fell in the desert? And to whom did God swear that they would never enter his rest if not to those who disobeyed? So we see that they were not able to enter, because of their unbelief. (Hebrews 3:17–19)

Now, the giving of the law at Mount Sinai was largely the occasion of this mixed experience of the Israelites. The law was indeed a revelation of the holiness and justice of God. Moreover, it was a divine standard of human character and conduct. But the law also revealed the sin of the people and stirred up the evil in their hearts to rebellion against God. It was not that the law was at fault. Indeed, the law was holy, just and good (Romans 7:12). Nor was the law in any wise a minister of sin. The fault lay, not at all with the law, but entirely with the people. It was powerless because of their weakness. As the reward of obedience the law promised life; but as the penalty of disobedience it threatened death.

> Keep my decrees and laws, for the man who obeys them will live by them. I am the Lord. (Leviticus 18:5)

> The soul who sins is the one who will die. The son will not share the guilt of the father, nor will the father share the guilt of the son. The righteousness of the righteous man will be credited to him, and the wickedness of the wicked will be charged against him. (Ezekiel 18:20)

Moreover, while the law upheld the standard of perfect righteousness, it also condemned any departure therefrom.

> All who rely on observing the law are under a curse, for it is written: "Cursed is everyone who does not continue to do everything written in the Book of the Law." (Galatians 3:10)

Since, however, none of the Israelites could keep the law, all were brought under its curse. Indeed, it was not the divine intention that the law should be kept. Its purpose was rather to include all under sin, in order that all might be saved by grace. So, when the law had done its work of revealing and condemning sin, the guilty and penitent Israelite came to the tabernacle with its priesthood and sacrifices, speaking of redemption by blood. Thus the law was a "schoolmaster" to bring sinners to Christ (Galatians 3:19–24).

New Testament counterpart

This mixed religious experience is also unfolded in the seventh chapter of Romans, which may be regarded as the New Testament counterpart of the wilderness journeying of the Israelites. The man there portrayed begins his Christian life like a happy child in his father's house. He has been saved and his life is full of joy and praise. But as soon as the revelation of God's holy law is made to his heart, the whole situation is changed.

Suddenly he becomes alive to a depth of iniquity within, whose presence he had not suspected. The old nature is laid bare in all its exceeding sinfulness and implacable enmity against God. And yet the man has the witness of the new divine life received through the birth from above. Let us look a little at this graphic portrayal, noticing the contending forces, the unequal contest and the hopeless defeat.

First, the contending forces. There are two opposing forces—the "I" of the natural life and the "I" of the spiritual life. The "I" of the natural life, "the old man," the Apostle variously calls "the sinful nature" (verse 5); "sin" (verse 17); "this body of death" (verse 24); and "I myself" (verse 25). On the other hand, he refers to the "I" of the spiritual life as "my inner being" (verse 22); "my mind" (verse 23, 25).

Second, the unequal contest. These two forces are opposite in character and antagonistic in operation. Jesus said, "Flesh gives birth to flesh, but the Spirit gives birth to spirit" (John 3:6). Like oil and water they do not mix, and they will not dwell peaceably together. Unceasingly they contend with each other for the mastery. The battleground is the Christian's heart, and the coveted prize is the Christian's life. But the contest is the equal, for while the new man of the heart struggles on alone, the old man is reenforced by the condemning power of the law and by the subtle wiles of Satan. It is true that the personality of the devil does not stand out prominently in the chapter, but the flesh is always one of his fields of operation. Moreover, in the unequal conflict with the flesh, fortified by the powers of darkness, the Christian is like a babe in a den of lions. Listen to some of the echoes of the warfare which show how bravely but helplessly the Christian struggles alone:

> What shall we say, then? Is the law sin? Certainly not! Indeed I would not have known what sin was except through the law. For I would not have known what coveting really was if the law had not said, "Do not covet." But sin, seizing the

opportunity afforded by the commandment, produced in me every kind of covetous desire. For apart from the law, sin is dead. Once I was alive apart from law; but when the commandment came, sin sprang to life and I died. (Romans 7:7–9).

We know that the law is spiritual; but I am unspiritual, sold as a slave to sin. I do not understand what I do. For what I want to do I do not do, but what I hate I do. And if I do what I do not want to do, I agree that the law is good. (verses 14–16)

For what I do is not the good I want to do; no, the evil I do not want to do—this I keep on doing. Now if I do what I do not want to do, it is no longer I who do it, but it is sin living in me that does it. So I find this law at work: When I want to do good, evil is right there with me. For in my inner being I delight in God's law; but I see another law at work in the members of my body, waging war against the law of my mind and making me a prisoner of the law of sin at work within my members. (verses 19–23)

Third, the hopeless defeat. Worn out at last by his weary struggle and fruitless efforts the Christian reluctantly gives up the unequal contest. He is unable, single handed, to subdue sin and conquer self. Hear his despairing cry, as he realizes that he is worsted in the fight:

What a wretched man I am! Who will rescue me from this body of death? (verse 24)

But his cry for reenforcements is heard, and just before he sinks under a threatening mortal blow of his enemy, the Deliverer appears on the scene, riding triumphantly over the foe. "Who is this coming from Edom,/ from Bozrah, with his garments stained crimson?/ Who is this, robed in splendor,/ striding forward in the greatness of his strength?/ It is I, speaking in righteousness, mighty to save" (Isaiah 63:1). Exultantly the Christian shouts, "Thanks be to God—through Jesus Christ our Lord!" (verse 25).

The meaning of this mixed experience

Now, just what does this mixed Christian experience mean? In a word, it means that we know Christ as our righteousness but not as our sanctification. We are converted, but we have not been made partakers of His holiness. Mighty is the transformation wrought by conversion and the new birth, but after all, these are only the initial experiences of the Christian life. We get a good deal, but we do not get everything, in conversion. Nor does conversion give us the germ, the embryo, out of which everything comes by a process of growth and development. Conversion imparts a new spiritual life and takes away the *love* of sin, but it does not change the old heart nor destroy the *power* of sin and self. Victory is assured only through the reception of the Holy Spirit and the indwelling of the risen Christ. But this involves a new experience, a second definite work of grace—a *crisis* as radical and revolutionary as the *crisis* of the new birth. In regeneration, we pass out of death into life, but in sanctification we pass out of the self-life into the Christ-life. In regeneration we receive a "new spirit." In sanctification we receive the Holy Spirit to indwell the "new spirit."

> I will give you a new heart and put a new spirit in you; I will remove from you your heart of stone and give you a heart of flesh. And I will put my Spirit in you and move you to follow my decrees and be careful to keep my laws. (Ezekiel 36:26–27)

Beloved, have you a mixed Christian experience—occasional victories but more frequent defeats in your struggles to subdue sin and conquer self? Then you are living in the wilderness. You are living in the seventh chapter of Romans. You have taken Christ as your Savior; you have become a child of God; you have received the witness of the Spirit; you are assured that you are "accepted in the Beloved." But you have come under the convicting power of the law, and in its light you have seen the depth of iniquity in your heart. Your efforts to please God have failed. Your struggles against temptation have worn you out. Have you become discouraged? Have you begun to wonder if this is all the Christian life means—unsatisfied longings and constant defeats? Have you about settled down in grim determination to fight out the battle as best you can? Has the despairing cry that was wrung from

Paul's anguished heart escaped your lips? "What a wretched man I am! Who will rescue me from this body of death?" (Romans 7:24).

Struggling child of God, I come to you as the bearer of good news. I tell you that just beyond the wilderness lies the Land of Promise where you will find rest and faith, victory instead of defeat, and complete satisfaction for every spiritual longing. I tell you that after the seventh chapter comes the eighth chapter of Romans, with its power over sin, its victory over self, and its fullness of blessing in Christ Jesus. The seventh chapter represents the best the believer can do alone; the eighth chapter represents the best Christ can do in the believer. The one is a sad story of darkness, disaster and despair; the other is a glorious record of light, life and liberty.

What makes all this vast difference? *The abiding presence and personal indwelling of the Holy Ghost.* In the seventh chapter, the Holy Ghost is not seen. The believer fights his battles alone against the triple power of the world, the flesh and the devil. But in the eighth chapter, the Holy Ghost is introduced. He personally indwells the believer, and gives him complete and glorious triumph over all his foes. In a word, in the seventh chapter the Holy Ghost is *with* the believer, but in the eighth chapter He is *within* him. The keynote of the seventh chapter of Romans is: "But I see another law at work in the members of my body, waging war against the law of my mind and making me a prisoner of the law of sin at work within my members" (verse 23).

The keynote of the eighth chapter, however, is:

. . . through Jesus Christ the law of the Spirit of
life set me free from the law of sin and death
(verse 2).

Beloved, may you leave the wilderness with its disappointment, defeat and despair, and enter the Land
of Promise with its milk and honey and corn and oil
and wine. May you move out of the seventh chapter
of Romans with its strain, struggle and sorrow, and
live in the eighth chapter with its rest and peace and
joy and power and triumph. Then through the indwelling of the blessed Comforter you will be victorious over sin, you will walk well pleasing unto God
and your life will be "one glad, sweet song."

The Poison of Sin

What, then, is the cause of the wilderness experience of the Christian, and what is the cure? These questions lead us at once into the heart of our theme. Briefly, we may say, the cause of the continual struggles and constant defeats after conversion is the satanic poison of sin. And the divine antidote for the satanic poison of sin is holiness. But what is sin?

The origin of sin is wrapped in obscurity. The Scriptures throw little light on the subject. Its introduction into the human race, however, is recorded in the third chapter of Genesis. It came in a four-fold way.

1. Through woman's deception (1 Timothy 2:14).
2. Through man's disobedience (Romans 5:9).
3. Through the serpent's enticement (Genesis 3:1–6).
4. Through Satan's malignity (Revelation 12:9).

Sin is a sad and terrible reality. This fact may be proved in three ways, namely: the teaching of Scripture, the testimony of mankind, and the witness of consciousness.

The teaching of the Scriptures is clear and unmistakable. For example:

> The next day John saw Jesus coming toward him and said, "Look, the Lamb of God, who takes away the sin of the world!" (John 1:29)

> For all have sinned and fall short of the glory of God. (Romans 3:23)

> But the Scripture declares that the whole world is a prisoner of sin, so that what was promised, being given through faith in Jesus Christ, might be given to those who believe. (Galatians 3:22)

The testimony of mankind to the fact of sin has been enacted into governmental legislation, has found recognition in every false religion, and is reflected in secular literature. The Toman philosopher Seneca said: "We have all sinned, some more and some less." The Roman poet Ovid wrote: "We all strive for what is forbidden." Goethe, the German poet and philosopher, confessed, "I see no fault which I myself might not have committed." A Chinese proverb runs, "There are two good men; one is dead, and the other is not yet born."

Consciousness gives no uncertain witness to the existence of sin. Every one knows that he is a sinner. No one of responsible years has ever lived free from the sense of personal guilt and moral defilement. Remorse of conscience for wrong doing hounds all the sons and daughters of Adam, and the sad and terrible consequences of sin are seen in the mental, moral and physical deterioration of the race.

But men do not agree with the testimony of God that sin is "exceeding sinful." There are those who go so far as to deny the very existence of sin. Others regard it as an accident or as an infirmity or disease. Some indeed call it "an amiable weakness." Others still, consider it as fatalism—a dread necessity to mortal existence. And not a few look upon sin as not altogether undesirable—as a sort of means of grace which is an aid to humility.

Now, in order to get a clear understanding of what sin is, let us examine the Scriptures.

I. Words for sin in the Old Testament.

1. The most common Hebrew word for sin signifies, literally, *to miss the mark.* In the original sense it is found in Judges 20:16: "Among all these soldiers there were seven hundred chosen men who were left-handed, each of whom could sling a stone at a hair and not miss." With its derivative forms this word means any moral deviation from the divine goal—a going beyond, a coming short or a falling aside.

> If you do what is right, will you not be accepted? But if you do not do what is right, sin is crouch-

ing at your door; it desires to have you, but you must master it. (Genesis 4:7)

Not only wilful and ignorant acts of sin but also evil states and dispositions are included within the scope of this Hebrew word.

2. Another word signifies bent or twisted (see Isaiah 21:3), and means moral perverseness or iniquity— "The distortion of nature caused by evil doing." Our English word *wrong*, i.e. that which is wrung out, of course, expresses the idea exactly.

> Then I acknowledged my sin to you and did not cover up my iniquity. I said, "I will confess my transgressions to the Lord"—and you forgave the guilt of my sin. (Psalm 32:5)

3. Another word, whose root signifies strong excitement, means the habit of evil, sin in the disposition. It is the opposite of righteousness.

> But the wicked are like the tossing sea, which cannot rest, whose waves cast up mire and mud. "There is no peace," says my God, "for the wicked." (Isaiah 57:20–21)

4. Another word is used for a revolt against rightful authority, that is, apostasy, or rebellion. It is commonly translated in the King James Version by the word "transgression."

> For I know my transgressions, and my sin is always before me. (Psalm 51:3).

5. Another word means to cross over a line, or, go beyond. It is usually rendered in the King James Version "transgress."

> Though you probe my heart and examine me at night, though you test me, you will find nothing; I have resolved that my mouth will not sin [transgress, KJV]. (Psalm 17:3)

6. Another word, which literally signifies to blow, represents sin in the aspect of vanity or nothingness.

> See, they are all false! Their deeds amount to nothing; their images are but wind and confusion. (Isaiah 41:29)

7. Still another word refers to the hardening of the heart—the highest degree of sin, stubbornness, obduracy.

> The Lord said to Moses, "When you return to Egypt, see that you perform before Pharaoh all the wonders I have given you the power to do. But I will harden his heart so that he will not let the people go." (Exodus 4:21)

That is, the Lord gave Pharaoh up to the hardening of his own heart. See also Joshua 11:20, First Samuel

6:6, Psalm 95:8, Proverbs 28:14, Mark 8:17, John 12:40, Romans 9:18 and Hebrews 3:8,15; 4:7.

All the Hebrew words that are translated sin or that mean sin in one form or another are far too numerous to be considered separately. Among those that remain the following may be mentioned: fault, Leviticus 4:3; go astray, Leviticus 4:13; wander, Ezekiel 34:6; backslide, Psalm 119:21; guilt or guilt offering, Isaiah 53:10; error or failure, Leviticus 19:17; trespass, Proverbs 10:12; mischief, Psalm 44:20; misery, Habakkuk 1:13.

II. Words for sin in the New Testament.

1. It is remarkable that in the New Testament Greek, as well as in the Old Testament Hebrew, the most common word for sin signifies, literally, to *miss the mark.* This word occurs 174 times, 71 times in the writings of the Apostle Paul. It expresses the state of iniquity as well as the act of sin.

> For all have sinned and fall short of the glory of God. (Romans 3:23)

Thus, sin is a "coming short of the glory of God."

> Therefore, just as sin entered the world through one man, and death through sin, and in this way death came to all men, because all sinned. (Romans 5:12)

2. Another word means the over-passing or over-stepping of a line of duty. It is always used of the "violation of a positive law, an express precept with an express sanction."

> And Adam was not the one deceived; it was the woman who was deceived and became a sinner. (1 Timothy 2:14)

3. Another word means a fall or failure—a falling where one should have stood.

> Brothers, if someone is caught in a sin, you who are spiritual should restore him gently. But watch yourself, or you also may be tempted. (Galatians 6:1).

This Greek word is variously translated in the King James Version as trespass, Matthew 6:14; sins, Ephesians 1:7; faults, James 5:16.

4. Another word means lawlessness, or anarchy.

> Everyone who sins breaks the law; in fact, sin is lawlessness. (1 John 3:4)

5. Another word means ignorance of what one should have known.

> But only the high priest entered the inner room, and that only once a year, and never without blood, which he offered for himself and for the

sins the people had committed in ignorance. (Hebrews 9:7)

6. Another word means the diminishing of that which one should have rendered in full.

The very fact that you have lawsuits among you means you have been completely defeated already. Why not rather be wronged? Why not rather be cheated? (1 Corinthians 6:7)

7. Another word means disobedience to a voice.

For if the message spoken by angels was binding, and every violation and disobedience received its just punishment, how shall we escape if we ignore such a great salvation? This salvation, which was first announced by the Lord, was confirmed to us by those who heard him. (Hebrews 2:2–3)

8. Still another word means a debt or an offense.

Forgive us our debts, as we also have forgiven our debtors. (Matthew 6:12)

Instances of other New Testament words which describe various forms of sin are: ungodliness, unrighteousness, Romans 1:18; lust, Romans 1:24; fornication, wickedness, covetousness, maliciousness, envy, deceit, malignity, murder, Romans 1:29, 31; enmity, Romans 8:7; flesh, adultery, uncleanness, lasciviousness, idolatry, witchcraft, hatred, variance, emulations, drunkenness, revelings, Galatians 5:19–21; evil, bitterness, wrath, anger, clamor, malice, Ephesians 4:31.

III. Scriptural definitions of sin.

There are in the Scriptures seven definitions of sin.

1. Proverbs 21:4: "Haughty eyes and a proud heart, the lamp of the wicked, are sin!"

2. Proverbs 24:9: "The schemes of folly are sin, and men detest a mocker."

3. John 16:8–9: "When he comes, he will convict the world of guilt in regard to sin and righteousness and judgment: in regard to sin, because men do not believe in me."

4. Romans 14:23: "But the man who has doubts is condemned if he eats, because his eating is not from faith; and everything that does not come from faith is sin."

5. James 4:17: "Anyone, then, who knows the good he ought to do and doesn't do it, sins."

6. 1 John 3:4: "Everyone who sins breaks the law; in fact, sin is lawlessness."

7. 1 John 5:17: "All wrongdoing is sin, and there is sin that does not lead to death."

IV. Theological definitions of sin.

The following definitions of sin are based on the Scriptures.

1. Sin is the transgression of, or lack of conformity to, the law of God.

2. Sin is inordinate desire, or concupiscence.
3. Sin is deficiency of love to God and man.
4. Sin is preference of self to God.
5. Sin is insubordination.
6. Sin is lack of conformity to God or His moral law in *act, disposition or state.*

V. Summary of scriptural teaching concerning sin.

A careful review of the teaching of the Scriptures concerning sin, which has here been presented, discloses the fact that sin may be viewed in four aspects, namely: toward God, toward the divine law, toward man and toward self.

First, toward God sin is either rebellion or failure to love Him supremely.

> **a.** Rebellion: "For rebellion is like the sin of divination, and arrogance like the evil of idolatry" (1 Samuel 15:23a).
> **b.** Failure to love Him supremely: "Love the Lord your God with all your heart and with all your soul and with all your strength" (Deuteronomy 6:5). (See also Mark 12:30).

Second, toward the divine law sin is either willful transgression or violations through ignorance.

> **a.** Willful transgression: "But anyone who sins defiantly, whether native-born or alien, blasphemes the Lord, and that person must be cut

off from his people" (Numbers 15:30). (See also Psalm 19:13).

b. Violation through ignorance: "But if just one person sins unintentionally, he must bring a year-old female goat for a sin offering" (Numbers 15:27). (See also Hebrews 9:7).

Third, toward man sin is either injustice of failure to love him as oneself.

a. Injustice: "Do not defraud your neighbor or rob him" (Leviticus 19:13). (See also Micah 6:8, Romans 1:18).

b. Failure to love him as oneself: "Do not seek revenge or bear a grudge against one of your people, but love your neighbor as yourself. I am the Lord" (Leviticus 19:18). (See also Mark 12:31).

Fourth, toward oneself sin is either selfishness or corruption.

a. Selfishness: That is "selfness" or the *self-life.* "If anyone would come after me he must deny himself and take up his cross and follow me" (Matthew 16:24). "The man who loves his life will lose it, while the man who hates his life in this world will keep it for eternal life" (John 12:25).

b. Corruption: "O Lord, open my lips, and my mouth will declare your praise" (Psalm 51:5).

CHAPTER

5

The Antidote for Sin—Holiness in the Old Testament.

The divine antidote for the satanic poison of sin is holiness. We have seen what sin is. Now let us try to understand what holiness is. We will study the subject, first in the Old Testament, and then in the New Testament.

Holiness is an attribute of God and a requirement of the people of God.

> The Lord said to Moses, "Speak to the entire assembly of Israel and say to them: 'Be holy because I, the Lord your God, am holy.'" (Leviticus 19:1–2)

> Consecrate yourselves and be holy, because I am the Lord your God. (Leviticus 20:7)

> Regard them as holy, because they offer up the food of your God. Consider them holy, because I

the Lord am holy—I who make you holy. (Leviticus 21:8)

For it is written: "Be holy because I am holy." (1 Peter 1:16)

As a divine attribute holiness is *purity*, and purity is essential to the Being of God. God is a Being who in nature, position and attributes is separate from all other beings, and is pure from every thought, feeling and deed of evil. The people of God, therefore, are to separate themselves from the world and from the things of the world and, like God, be pure from every thought, feeling and deed of evil. Thus, as a requirement of believers, holiness or sanctification—the words have the same meaning and are interchangeable in use—is *purity*. When he takes Christ to be "made unto him sanctification," the child of God becomes partaker of the purity of God in Christ through the personal indwelling of the Holy Spirit.

I. The *signification* of the word for holiness.

The Hebrew word commonly translated holy or holiness in the Authorized Version is *Kadesh*. In its various forms its signifies *the being set apart for the work of God*. The nearest English equivalent of the Hebrew word is *sacred*. Says Canon Girlestone: "The terms 'sanctification' and 'holiness' are now used so frequently to represent moral and spiritual qualities, that they hardly convey to the reader the idea of the position or relationship as existing between God and some person or thing consecrated to Him; yet this appears to be the real meaning of the word." *Separation for service*—this is the fundamental idea of the Hebrew word *Kadesh.*

II. The *Application* of the word for holiness.

The Hebrew word has a varied application.

First, to places and objects. For example:

1. Heaven is holy (Psalm 20:6).
2. Mount Sinai was holy (Psalm 68:17).
3. The lad of Canaan was holy (Zechariah 2:13).
4. The ground where Jehovah revealed Himself to Moses was holy (Exodus 3:5).
5. The king's chapel was holy (Amos 7:13).
6. The house or field set apart for God was holy (Leviticus 27:14, 16).
7. The city of Jerusalem was holy (Nehemiah 11:1).
8. The walls and gates of the city were holy (Nehemiah 3:1).
9. The tabernacle was holy (Exodus 29:43).
10. The temple was holy (1 Kings 9:3).
11. The hill of Zion was holy (Psalm 2:6).
12. The camp of Israel was holy (Deuteronomy 23:14).
13. The sanctuary was holy (Exodus 25:8).
14. The altar was holy (Exodus 29:36).

15. The gifts and offerings placed on the altar were holy (Exodus 28:38; 29:27).

Second, to times. For example:

1. The Sabbath was holy (Genesis 2:3; Exodus 20:8, 11).
2. The day set apart for a fast was holy (Joel 1:14).
3. The 50th year of jubilee was holy (Leviticus 25:10).

Third, to persons. For example:

1. The first-born of Israel was holy (Exodus 13:2).
2. The people of Israel were holy (Deuteronomy 7:6).
3. The assembly of Israel was holy (Psalm 89:7; Joel 2:16).
4. The "man of God" was holy (2 Kings 4:9).
5. The prophet Jeremiah was holy (Jeremiah 1:5).
6. The guests at a sacrificial feast were holy (Zephaniah 1:7).
7. The saints, or people dedicated to God, whether angels or men, were holy (Job 1:5; 15:15; Psalm 16:3; 34:9; Isaiah 4:3; Daniel 4:13; 7:18, 21–22, 25, 27; 8:13, 24; Zechariah 14:5).

Now, when we examine closely the meaning of the sanctification of places, objects and persons, we find that in every one of the instances mentioned the underlying thought is *contact with God.* Thus, heaven is holy, because there is the throne of God. Mount Sinai is holy, because there God gave Israel His law. The land of Canaan is holy, because God has chosen it as the permanent possession of His people. Jerusalem is holy, because God has chosen it for the manifestation of His name. The temple was holy, because therein the symbol of God's presence was visible. The Sabbath was holy, because God had chosen it as His day of rest. Israel was holy, because from among all nations God had chosen this nation to be His "peculiar people." The priests were holy, because they ministered in the service of the Lord. The prophets were holy, because they spoke in the name of the Lord. And the kings were holy, because they ruled in the stead of the Lord. Indeed, in every example of holiness in the Old Testament this fundamental idea of *contact with God* is prominent.

Besides the application of the word holy or holiness to places, objects and persons, the expressions are used, as we have already seen, of the Divine Being. Thus God is holy (Joshua 29:19); Jehovah, or the Lord God is holy (1 Samuel 6:20); the Divine Spirit is holy (Psalm 51:11; Isaiah 63:10–11. We may also refer to such expressions as the following:

Holy and awesome is his name. (Psalm 111:9)

Holy, holy, holy, is the Lord Almighty. (Isaiah 6:3)

They will keep my name holy;
>   they will acknowledge the holiness of the Holy
>   One of Jacob. (Isaiah 29:23b)

Your statutes stand firm;
>   holiness adorns your house. (Psalm 93:5)

Rejoice in the Lord, you who are righteous,
>   and praise his holy name. (Psalm 97:12)

The Holy One of Israel. (2 Kings 19:22; Psalm 71:22; Isaiah 10:17; 49:7)

Splendor of his holiness. (1 Chronicles 26:29; Psalm 29:2; 96:9)

Holy to the Lord. (Exodus 28:36; 39:30)

III. The *use* of the word holiness.

The use of the word holiness or sanctification in the Old Testament is two-fold, namely: ceremonial and moral. Ceremonial holiness is official holiness—the holiness of position or relationship. Moral holiness is personal holiness—the holiness of renewed character and righteous conduct. Ceremonial holiness belongs to both persona and things; while moral holiness belongs only to persons.

First, Ceremonial Holiness.

Ceremonial holiness is the holiness of an office—the

external holiness of position or relationship. In its essence it is *sacredness*. It is the only kind of holiness that can belong to things. Thus, the city of Jerusalem, the Sabbath day, and the temple and all its furniture, even down to the implements of the altar, were holy or sacred because they had all been set apart for the worship and service of Jehovah.

On the other hand, the whole nation of Israel, and all the prophets, priests and kings were holy because in a special and peculiar way they had been brought into direct *contact with Jehovah*. Thus, the kings were the vice-regents of God, and as the chosen rulers in His stead, were holy. Again, the priests were the ministers of sacrifice and worship, and as the chosen mediators between Jehovah and Israel, were holy. Again, the prophets were primarily preachers of righteousness, and as the chosen vehicles of divine truth, were holy. And finally, the Israelites had been redeemed out of the house of bondage, and as the chosen people of God, were holy.

Now, *as a nation* Israel was ceremonially holy, but not morally holy. Separated from all other nations, dedicated to God by a solemn covenant and appointed to become the channel of blessing to the whole earth, the Hebrew race had been brought into special and direct *contact with Jehovah*. The law of Moses exacted absolute conformity to its lofty requirements. And these requirements covered the inward motive as well as the outward action. Perfect holiness was enjoined upon the people in all their relations to Jehovah and in all their dealings with one another. But the obedience that Israel rendered was to the letter and not to the spirit of the law. There was outward conformation of conduct but not inward transformation of character. In other words, the holiness of the people, as a people, was ceremonial and not moral.

Take for example, the teaching of the book of Leviticus. Its keynote is: "A holy God will have a holy people." In chapters 19 and 20 there is a summary of sundry laws concerning the relation of the people to Jehovah and their relation to one another. These laws are searching, affecting character as well as conduct. Can we for one moment think that God would have been satisfied with anything less than perfect obedience to these and all other laws enjoining righteousness and godliness? And yet, not alone in moral holiness, but in ceremonial holiness as well, the people as a nation signally failed. What other meaning, indeed, have the sacrificial offerings and ritual cleansings of the Levitical system? Moreover, it was expected by God that Israel would fail at every point. This is seen by the fact that provision was made for failure in the Mosaic sacrifices and ritual purifications.

Thus, it is far from the truth to hold that as a nation the people of Israel were morally holy. That is, that *every member of the Hebrew race had experienced a spiritual renewal of character.* Indeed, it was their lack of moral holiness—the possession of an evil heart of unbelief and rebellion—that was the cause of the failure of the people even in ceremonial holiness.

> For this people's heart has become calloused;
>   they hardly hear with their ears,
>   and they have closed their eyes.

> Otherwise they might see with their eyes,
>   hear with their ears,
>   understand with their hearts
>   and turn, and I would heal them. (Acts 28:27)

And with whom was he angry for 40 years? Was it not with those who sinned, whose bodies fell in the desert? And to whom did God swear that they would never enter into his rest if not to those who disobeyed? So we see that they were not able to enter, because of their unbelief. (Hebrews 3:17–19)

Second, Moral Holiness.

Moral holiness is *purity.* It has elsewhere been defined as personal holiness—the holiness of renewed character and of righteous conduct. These two elements belong together, the one being the seed and the other the fruit of a transformed life. Moral holiness belongs only to persons.

While Israel *as a nation* was only ceremonially holy, *individual Israelites* were morally holy. The Hebrew people, as we have seen, fell short even of the full requirements of the ceremonial law. However, innumerable members of the race satisfied God by becoming partakers of His holiness through a spiritual transformation of their hearts and lives.

The testimony of the Old Testament Scriptures is clear both to the fact that Jehovah required His people to be holy and to the fact that individual Israelites earnestly yearned for conformity to the divine will in

heart and life. For proof of this statement we do not
need to go outside the 51st Psalm:

> Surely you desire truth in the inner parts;
>   you teach me wisdom in the inmost place.
> (verse 6)

> You do not delight in sacrifice, or I would bring
>   it;
>   you do not take pleasure in burnt offerings.
> The sacrifices of God are a broken spirit;
>   a broken and contrite heart,
>   O God, you will not despise. (verses 16–17)

> Have mercy on me, O God,
>   according to your unfailing love;
> according to your great compassion
>   blot out my transgressions.
> Wash away all my iniquity
>   and cleanse me from my sin.
> For I know my transgressions
>   and my sin is always before me. (verses 1–3)

> Cleanse me with hyssop, and I will be clean;
>   wash me, and I will be whiter than snow.
> (verse 7)

> Create in me a pure heart, O God,
>   and renew a steadfast spirit within me.
> (verse 10)

The following passages of like tenor may also be ex-

amined: Psalm 24:3–5; Isaiah 57:15; Jeremiah 33:8;
Ezekiel 36:25, 33; Malachi 1:11; 3:3.

Now, the Lord always meets and satisfies the yearn-
ing desire for holiness which He Himself creates. Can
we doubt, for example, that King David who uttered
this earnest prayer did not have the desire of his heart
fulfilled?

> As the deer pants for streams of water,
>   so my soul pants for you, O God.
> My soul thirsts for God, for the living God.
>   When can I go and meet with God?
>   (Psalm 42:1–2)

See also Psalm 63:1–2.

The Lord has always reserved for Himself a godly
seed, a righteous people, a holy remnant. "Know that
the Lord has set apart the godly for himself;/ the Lord
will hear when I call him" (Psalm 4:3).

Let us take a rapid survey of Old Testament history,
beginning with the infancy of the race. Righteous
Abel was the first of the line of the godly seed. To take
his place God raised up Seth, from whom descended
holy Enoch, who "walked with God; then he was no
more, because God took him away" (Genesis 5:24).
God-fearing Noah "in holy fear built an ark to save
his family. By his faith he condemned the world and
became heir of the righteousness that comes by faith"
(Hebrews 11:7). Abraham, the friend of God, "by
faith he made his home in the promised land like a
stranger in a foreign country; he lived in tents, as did
Isaac and Jacob, who were heirs with him of the same

promise" (Hebrews 11:9). We could also look at many others: Sarah, Joseph, Moses, the triumphant hosts of the Israelites at the Red Sea and before the walls of Jericho, Rahab, Gideon, Barak, Samson, Jephthah, David and Samuel and the prophets.

> Who through faith conquered kingdoms, administered justice, and gained what was promised; who shut the mouths of lions, quenched the fury of the flames, and escaped the edge of the sword; whose weakness was turned to strength; and who became powerful in battle and routed foreign armies. (Hebrews 11:33–34)

And lest we should think that his roll of heroes was exhaustive instead of representative of a "great cloud of witnesses," the writer adds:

> Women received back their dead, raised to life again. Others were tortured and refused to be released, so that they might gain a better resurrection. Some faced jeers and flogging, while still others were chained and put in prison. They were stoned; they were sawed in two; they were put to death by the sword. They went about in sheepskins and goatskins, destitute, persecuted and mistreated—the world was not worthy of them. They wandered in deserts and mountains, and in caves and holes in the ground. These were condemned for their faith, yet none of them received what had been promised. God had planned something better for us so that only

together with us would they be made perfect.
(Hebrews 11:35–40)

This glorious 11th chapter of Hebrews covers the
long period of over 4,000 years from Abel to Malachi.
How large a "great cloud of witnesses" there was to
the spiritual worship of Jehovah no one can tell. In his
day Elijah believed that he was the only faithful fol-
lower of the Lord, yet God assured him that He had
reserved for Himself 7,000 in Israel who had not
bowed the knee unto Baal, nor kissed his image in
idolatrous worship (1 Kings 19:18). Just before the
Old Testament closes and the long night of prophetic
silence is ushered in, we have this exquisite picture of
the "little flock" that shall yet inherit the kingdom of
God.

> Then those who feared the Lord talked with each
> other, and the Lord listened and heard. A scroll
> of remembrance was written in his presence con-
> cerning those who feared the Lord and honored
> his name. "They will be mine," says the Lord Al-
> mighty, "in the day when I will make up my
> treasured possession. I will spare them, just as in
> compassion a man spares his son who serves
> him." (Malachi 3:16–17)

IV. The *Mode* of holiness.

The mode of holiness was the means or process
whereby a person or thing became holy. In a word,

holiness was brought about by *contact with God.* In the case of ceremonial holiness the contact was *external* and *official,* and the holiness consisted in a scene of *sacredness* that invested the person or thing. In the case of moral holiness the contact was *spiritual* and *personal,* and the holiness consisted in a scene of *sacredness* that invested the person or thing. The contact was also spiritual and personal in the case of moral holiness but the holiness consisted in *purity* of heart and life—the very nature of God being imparted to the devout worshiper.

First, Ceremonial Holiness.

In the ritual of ceremonial holiness four elements were employed: water, fire, blood and oil. These emblems were typical: the blood of the redemptive work of Christ; and the water, fire and oil of the separating, purifying and consecrating work of the Holy Spirit.

Objects were regarded as clean when passed through either water or fire.

> Then Eleazer the priest said to the soldiers who had gone into battle, "This is the requirement of the law that the Lord gave Moses: Gold, silver, bronze, iron, tin, lead and anything else that can withstand fire must be put through that water. On the seventh day wash your clothes and you will be clean. Then you may come into the camp." (Numbers 31:21–23)

Water, blood and oil were applied to persons. The

process of ritual sanctification in the Old Testament is clearly seen in the cleansing of the leper, the consecration of the priests and the water of separation.

I. The Cleansing of the Leper (Leviticus 14).

In the cleansing of the leper there were three steps: first, the healing of the disease; second, the announcement of cleanness by the priest; and third, the rites of cleansing. Here we are concerned only with the rites of cleansing. There was a five-fold process.

1. Sacrifice.
Two birds were taken. One was slain, and the other, dipped in its blood with the cedar wood and the scarlet and the hyssop, was released in the open field. The typical significance of this rite is set forth in Romans 4:25: "He was delivered over to death for our sins and was raised to life for our justification."

2. Cleansing by water.
All the hair of the leper was shaved, and his body and clothes were then washed in water to symbolized his complete separation from his former life and habits.

3. Sprinkling with blood seven times.
Seven times the leper was sprinkled with blood by the priest to represent his *entire cleansing*. Then some blood was put upon the tip of his right ear, the thumb of his right hand and the

great toe of his right foot as a type of the *redemption* of all his faculties and powers.

4. Sprinkling with oil seven times.

The same process was repeated with the anointing oil in token that all the members of the cleansed leper's body, the faculties of his mind, the powers of his soul and his daily walk and habits of life were solemnly set apart in *dedication to God.*

5. The rest of the oil.

Lastly, a rite of deep spiritual significance was performed. We read: "The rest of the oil in his palm the priest shall put on the head of the one to be cleansed, to make atonement for him before the Lord" (Leviticus 14:29). This was the "residue of the oil." And its being poured over the head of the cleansed leper may be taken as a symbol of the *fullness* of the Holy Ghost, just as the application of the oil may be taken as an emblem of the *reception* of the Holy Ghost. The "seven times" of the sprinkled blood and the sprinkled oil represents completeness.

II. The Consecration of the Priests (Exodus 28:41–29:24; Leviticus 8:1–9:24).

The ritual sanctification of the priests, or their dedication to office, was substantially the same as the process for the cleansing of the leper: sacrifice, washing, the sprinkling of the blood and the sprinkling of the oil. One feature of the solemn service, however, was unique. That was *the filling of the hand.* The act of consecration included a part of the sacrifice being put in the priest's hand, waved, and then taken to the altar. The Hebrew word translated "consecrated," as used in this rite, means *to fill the hand.* (See Exodus 28:41; Leviticus 8:27–28). Spiritually, the meaning is that after we have been separated from sin and dedicated to God, and have received the Holy Spirit, we are appointed to fruitful service. We are not to be idle in the vineyard of the Lord nor spend our time in holy contemplation. But God fills our hands with loving ministries to Himself and to the sinful and needy. Jesus said: "You did not choose me, but I chose you and appointed you to go and bear fruit—fruit that will last. Then the Father will give you whatever you ask in my name" (John 15:16).

III. The Water of Separation (Numbers 19).

The ordinance or the red heifer differed materially from the law of the leper's cleansing and the ritual of the priest's consecration. The law of leprosy provided for the cleansing from a loathsome disease. The ritual of consecration marked the solemn setting apart of a priest to his holy office. The water of separation, on the other hand, was applied to the ordinary Israelite, who during the course of his daily walk might become ceremonially defiled. There were four parts to the ordinances, namely: the killing of the red heifer, the seven-fold sprinkling of its blood, the preparation and preservation of the ashes as a memorial before the Lord and the act of cleansing from defilement by sprinkling the unclean object or person with a kind of lye formed by mixing some of the ashes with water.

Spiritually, this impressive ordinance teaches us God's way of cleansing His children from the defilement of daily contact with evil. The slaying of the red heifer and the seven-fold sprinkling of the blood are a type of the atonement of Christ. The ashes kept in a clean place typify the finished work of our Lord as the perpetual ground of our daily cleansing. The water is a symbol of the Holy Ghost.

The deep significance of all this in Christian experience is beautifully set forth, both pictorially and doctrinally, in the 13th chapter of John. While in the upper room at the passover feast, Jesus girded Himself with a towel, and pouring water in a basin began to wash the disciple's feet. In Oriental countries, where sandals are worn, the feet become dusty, and frequent washings of the feet are necessary. Feet washing was an act of hospitality, which was customarily performed by servants. The fact that Jesus undertook this menial office was a proof of His own humility and a lesson in humility for the disciples.

To Peter, who objected to his feet being washed, the Master said: "A person who has a bath needs only to wash his feet; his whole body is clean. And you are clean, though not every one of you (John 13:10). Here two Greek verbs are used. The first, translated "washed," is *louo* and means the bathing of the entire body. The second, rendered "wash," is *nipto* and means the washing of a part of the body. Literally, we may read: "A person who is *bathed* needs only to *wash* his feet; his whole body is clean." That is, a man bathed himself in the morning, but throughout the day he washed his feet whenever they required it. So Jesus taught that after regeneration, which cannot be repeated, a daily cleansing of the believer's walk and conversation takes place. This the Holy Ghost accomplishes by means of the blood of Christ, and through the agency of the Word of God.

> Christ loved the church and gave himself up for her to make her holy, cleansing her by the washing with water through the word. (Ephesians 5:25–26)

> He saved us, not because of righteous things we had done, but because of his mercy. He saved us through the washing of rebirth and renewal by the Holy Spirit. (Titus 3:5)

> But if we walk in the light, as he is in the light, we have fellowship with one another, and the blood of Jesus, his Son, purifies us from all sin. (1 John 1:7)

The Greek verb translated "purifies" is in the present tense; literally, it means *keeps purifying*.

Second, Moral Holiness.

As we have seen, the means whereby a person or thing becomes holy is *contact with God.* If the contact with God is external and official, the holiness is ceremonial in nature, and consists in a sense of sacredness with which the person or thing is invested. On the other hand, if the contact with God is internal and spiritual, the result is moral holiness, which consists of *purity* of heart and life—the very purity of God Himself imparted to the devout believer. We are now to inquire more carefully into the process whereby moral holiness is secured.

How were the Old Testament worthies in the long line from Abel to Malachi sanctified in character and conduct? We have said *by a vital and spiritual contact with God.* But this statement calls for some consideration.

Of course, in its inner nature the mode of moral holiness is not clear. Mystery surrounds all the works of God, especially the operations of divine grade upon the human heart. The Apostle Paul declared: "Beyond all question, the mystery of godliness is great:/ He appeared in a body" (1 Timothy 3:16). And this statement is just as true of Christ's being manifested in us as it is of God's being manifested in Christ.

> To them God has chosen to make known among the Gentiles the glorious riches of this mystery, which is Christ in you, the hope of glory. (Colossians 1:27)

The new birth is a profound mystery. Jesus said:

> The wind blows wherever it pleases. You hears its sound, but you cannot tell where it comes from

or where it is going. So it is with everyone born of the Spirit. (John 3:8)

Sanctification is also a profound mystery. We cannot trace the inner process whereby a soul becomes partaker of the divine holiness. Particularly is this true in the Old Testament, where so little comparatively is revealed concerning the hidden working upon hearts and lives of the Spirit of God. We know, however, that God has but one way of salvation. Consequently, we may say that the mode of moral holiness in the Old Testament was three-fold, namely: the cross of Christ, the work of the Spirit and the faith of the Israelite.

The Cross of Christ

The Levitical system of sacrificial offerings and ritual cleansings was typical of Christ and His redemptive work. The individual Israelite was saved through a Savior who was to come, just as the sinner today is saved through a Savior who has come. In one case the redemption was prophetic; in the other case it is historic. So, too, the Old Testament saints were sanctified by the cross. The finished work of Christ, typified in the offerings, was the ground of their moral cleansing.

The Work of the Spirit

Of course, dispensationally speaking, the Holy Spirit bore a relation to Old Testament times quite different from what He bears to the present age. The divine Spirit did not indwell the congregation of Israel

as He indwells the Church of God. Indeed, an out-
pouring of the Spirit, such as was witnessed at Pentecost, was distinctly foretold (Isaiah 32:14–17;
Ezekiel 36:25–27; Joel 2:28–32; Zechariah 12:10).
Yet the Holy Spirit as a person was with and among
the people of Israel (Genesis 6:3; Psalm 51:2; Isaiah
63:10; Ezekiel 11:5; Haggai 2:5).

In particular there was a four-fold work of the Spirit
of God:

(a). He came *upon* men. That is, He clothed
Himself with them. Of this Gideon is an example (Judges 6:34).

(b). He came *upon* men *mightily*. That is, He
forced them into something, so to speak. Of this
Samson is an example (Judges 15:14).

(c). He *equipped* men and *filled* them for specific
service. Of this Bezaleel (Exodus 31:2–3), Cyrus
(Isaiah 45:1) and Zerubabel (Zechariah 4:6) are
examples.

(d). He *indwelt* men. Of only Joseph and Joshua,
however, is this fact recorded (Genesis 41:38;
Numbers 27:18; see also Daniel 5:2).

Now, it is with this last operation of the Holy
Ghost—indwelling men—that the work of sanctification is to be specifically connected. While it is true
that God's Spirit is said, in so many words, to have indwelt only Joseph and Joshua, may we not take these
men as representatives of a large class, perhaps an innumerable multitude of saints, such as Abel, Enoch,
Noah, Abraham and the patriarchs, and the long line

of godly priests, prophets and kings? Is it not safe to say that it was the privilege and experience of individual Israelites *then*, as it is the privilege and experience of believers now, to have the gracious working of the divine Spirit not only *upon* them but *within* them as well? Yet in the former dispensation the Holy Spirit seems to have visited men occasionally—at least in some cases He came and went. But in the present age, when we definitely receive Him, He comes to abide *forever*. Surely, then, we may believe that the Old Testament saints were made partakers of the purity of God—that is, were sanctified in heart and life—by the gracious inworking of the divine Spirit.

The Faith of the Israelite

It is the clear teaching of the 11th chapter of Hebrews that the long line of Old Testament worthies from Abel onward were saved and sanctified by faith. It was by faith—faith in the Word of Jehovah, in the redemptive value of the sacrifices and in the gracious inworking of the Spirit—that their lives were spiritually transformed and they themselves wrought mighty achievements for God. For it was true then, as it is true now: "And without faith it is impossible to please God, because anyone who comes to him must believe that he exists and that he rewards those who earnestly seek him" (Hebrews 11:6).

CHAPTER

6

The Antidote for Sin—Holiness in the New Testament

Having studied the subject of holiness in the Old Testament, let us now turn to the New Testament. Here we shall find the teaching deeper and richer, inasmuch as the dispensation of grace is in advance of the dispensation of law. "For the law was given through Moses; grace and truth came through Jesus Christ" (John 1:17).

I. The *Signification* of the words for holiness in the New Testament.

There are five Greek words from the same root translated holy or holiness (sanctify or sanctification) in the New Testament, namely: a verb—*hagiazo*; an adjective—*hagios*; and three nouns—*hagiasmos, hagiotes,* and *hagiosune*. They are all practically synonymous in meaning with the Hebrew word *kadesh*. Thus the verb *hagiazo* signifies primarily the sacredness, veneration or hallowedness that a person, place or object possesses by virtue of *contact with God.* In the King James Version the verb is translated by the words holy, hallow and sanctify.

II. The *Application* of the words for holiness.

As in the Old Testament, there is a wide application of the words for holiness in the New Testament.

For example: first, to places. The city of Jerusalem, the sanctuary of the temple and the temple of believers are holy (Matthew 4:5; 24:15; Ephesians 2:21). Second, to objects. The covenant of God, the Scriptures and the law are holy (Luke 1:72; Romans 1:2; 7:12). Third, to persons. Believers, often called saints in the epistles, the prophets and the angels are holy (Hebrews 3:1; 1 Corinthians 1:2; 2 Corinthians 1:1; Acts 3:21; Revelation 14:10).

Besides these and many other instances the word *holy* is applied to the divine Being, thus: the Father is holy (John 17:2); the Son is holy (Mark 1:24; Luke 1:35; 1 John 2:20); and the divine Spirit is holy (Matthew 3:2; Acts 13:2; Romans 15:16).

As in the Old Testament, in every instance of the occurrence of the word holy in the New Testament, whether applied to person, places or objects, the fundamental idea of *contact with God* is prominent.

III. The *Use* of the words for holiness.

The full discussion of the nature of ceremonial and moral holiness in the Old Testament makes it unnecessary to go over the ground again in detail. The fundamental principles are the same. The Greek words for holiness or sanctification are employed with the wide range of meaning of the Hebrew word: separation from sin, dedication to God and consecration to service—in a word, moral and ceremonial holiness. If the contact with God is material, the holiness is ceremonial. If the contact is spiritual, the holiness is moral.

First, Ceremonial Holiness.

Both ceremonial and moral holiness are taught in the Old and in the New Testament—but with this difference: in the Old Testament the emphasis is on ceremonial holiness, while in the New Testament it is on moral holiness.

1. The Ceremonial Holiness of Things.

The following are a few illustrative examples:

> You blind fools! Which is greater: the gold, or the temple that makes the gold sacred? You also say, "If anyone swears by the altar, it means nothing; but if anyone swears by the gift on it, he is bound by his oath." You blind men! Which is greater: the gift, or the altar that makes the gift sacred? (Matthew 23:17–19)

> For everything God created is good, and nothing is to be rejected if it is received with thanksgiving, because it is consecrated by the word of God and prayer. (1 Timothy 4:4–5)

2. The Ceremonial Holiness of Persons.

There is a striking example of the ceremonial holiness of persons in First Corinthians 7:14: "For the unbelieving husband has been sanctified through his wife, and the unbelieving wife has been sanctified through her believing husband. Otherwise your children would be unclean, but as it is, they are holy." On this passage Meyer's comment is: "The Christian sanctity affects even the nonbelieving partner in a marriage and so passes over to him that he does not remain a profane person, but through the intimate union of wedded life becomes partaker (as if by a sacred contagion) of the higher divinely constituted character of his consort." And Dr. Lias, in the Cambridge Bible, adds: "This principle applies also to the children of such a marriage. The sanctity, *i.e.*, the consecration, of the parent possessing the life of Christ, and living in holy wedlock with an unbelieving husband or wife, descends to the child, which from its birth *may be regarded* as 'holy to the Lord.' "

Second, Moral Holiness.

We will notice, in the first place, the holiness of Christ and, in the second place, the holiness of believers.

1. The Holiness of Christ.

What about the one whom the Father set apart as his very own and sent into the world? Why

then do you accuse me of blasphemy because I
said, "I am God's Son"? (John 10:36)

For them I sanctify myself, that they too may be
truly sanctified. (John 17:19)

In these two passages, with reference to our Lord,
the expressions "set apart" and "sanctify" can be understood only of His setting apart for the work of
redemption. Says a great English scholar: "We ought
to interpret these passages in the light of the
sanctification of the priest, the altar and all the holy
things of the older dispensation which were the
shadows, while Christ was the substance. The Lord
was 'set apart' from the foundation of the world for
the work of redemption, and His incarnation, temptations and sufferings were the processes whereby His
atoning death was prepared for and rendered valid."

In this connection we may examine, in passing, a
peculiar use of the word *sanctify* in the Scriptures,
which refers exclusively to God Himself.

Moses then said to Aaron, "This is what the Lord
spoke of when he said: 'Among those who approach me I will show myself holy; in the sight
of all the people I will be honored.' " (Leviticus
10:3)

But in your hearts set apart Christ as Lord. (1
Peter 3:15a)

In these passages the word sanctify seems to be used

in a declarative sense, so to speak; that is, to hold God in reverence and worship and honor Him.

2. The Holiness of Believers.

The following are among the most important passages in the New Testament, which refer to the sanctification of believers in heart and life.

> Sanctify them by the truth; your word is truth. (John 17:17)

> . . . that they may receive forgiveness of sins and a place among those who are sanctified by faith in me. (Acts 26:18)

> . . . so now offer them in slavery to righteousness leading to holiness. (Romans 6:19)

> But now that you have been set free from sin and have become slaves to God, the benefit you reap leads to holiness, and the result is eternal life. (Romans 6:22)

> To the church of God in Corinth, to those sanctified in Christ Jesus and called to be holy. (1 Corinthians 1:2a)

> It is because of him that you are in Christ Jesus, who has become for us wisdom from God—that is, our righteousness, holiness and redemption. (1 Corinthians 1:30)

And that is what some of you were. But you were washed, you were sanctified, you were justified in the name of the Lord Jesus Christ and by the Spirit of our God. (1 Corinthians 6:11)

Since we have these promises, dear friends, let us purify ourselves from everything that contaminates body and spirit, perfecting holiness out of reverence for God. (2 Corinthians 7:1)

Husbands, love your wives, just as Christ loved the church and gave himself up for her to make her holy, cleansing her by the washing with water through the word. (Ephesians 5:25–26)

May he strengthen your hearts so that you will be blameless and holy in the presence of our God and Father when our Lord Jesus comes with all his holy ones. (1 Thessalonians 3:13)

It is God's will that you should be sanctified: that you should avoid sexual immorality; that each of you should learn to control his own body in a way that is holy and honorable. . . . For God did not call us to be impure, but to live a holy life. (1 Thessalonians 4:3–4, 7)

May God himself, the God of peace, sanctify you through and through. May your whole spirit, soul and body be kept blameless at the coming of our Lord Jesus Christ. (1 Thessalonians 5:23)

But we ought always to thank God for you, brothers loved by the Lord, because from the beginning God chose you to be saved through the sanctifying work of the Spirit and through belief in the truth. (2 Thessalonians 2:13)

But women will be saved through childbearing— if they continue in faith, love and holiness with propriety. (1 Timothy 2:15)

If a man cleanses himself from the latter, he will be an instrument for noble purposes, made holy, useful to the Master and prepared to do any good work. (2 Timothy 2:21)

Both the one who makes men holy and those who are made holy are of the same family. So Jesus is not ashamed to call them brothers. (Hebrews 2:11)

And by that will, we have been made holy through the sacrifice of the body of Jesus Christ once for all. (Hebrews 10:10)

Because by one sacrifice he has made perfect forever those who are being made holy. (Hebrews 10:14)

How much more severely do you think a man deserves to be punished who has trampled the Son of God under foot, who has treated as an unholy thing the blood of the covenant that sanctified him, and who has insulted the Spirit of grace? (Hebrews 10:29)

Our fathers disciplined us for a little while as they thought best; but God disciplines us for our good, that we may share in his holiness. (Hebrews 12:10)

Make every effort to live in peace with all men and to be holy; without holiness no one will see the Lord. (Hebrews 12:14)

And so Jesus also suffered outside the city gate to make the people holy through his own blood. (Hebrews 13:12)

Who have been chosen according to the foreknowledge of God the Father, through the sanctifying work of the Spirit, for obedience to Jesus Christ and sprinkling by his blood. (1 Peter 1:2)

Jude, a servant of Jesus Christ and a brother of James, to those who have been called [are sanctified, KJV], who are loved by God the Father and kept by Jesus Christ. (Jude 1)

To rescue us from the hand of our enemies, and to enable us to serve him without fear in holiness and righteousness before him all our days. (Luke 1:74–75)

And to put on the new self, created to be like God in true righteousness and holiness. (Ephesians 4:24)

When Peter saw this, he said to them: "Men of Israel, why does this surprise you? Why do you stare at us as if by our own power or godliness we had made this man walk?" (Acts 3:12)

Likewise, teach the older women to be reverent in the way they live. (Titus 2:3a)

You are already clean because of the word I have spoken to you. (John 15:3)

But if we walk in the light, as he is in the light, we have fellowship with one another, and the blood of Jesus, his Son, purifies us from all sin. (1 John 1:7)

If we confess our sins, he is faithful and just and will forgive us our sins and purify us from all un-righteousness. (1 John 1:9)

Blessed are the pure in heart, for they will see God. (Matthew 5:8)

The goal of this command is love, which comes from a pure heart and a good conscience and a sincere faith. (1 Timothy 1:5)

. . . keep yourself pure. (1 Timothy 5:22b)

Flee the evil desires of youth, and pursue righteousness, faith, love and peace, along with those who call on the Lord out of a pure heart. (2 Timothy 2:22)

Now that you have purified yourselves by obeying the truth so that you have sincere love for your brothers, love one another deeply, from the heart. (1 Peter 1:22)

Everyone who has this hope in him purifies himself, just as he is pure. (1 John 3:3)

He made no distinction between us and them, for he purified their hearts by faith. (Acts 15:9)

Have nothing to do with godless myths and old wives' tales; rather, train yourself to be godly. (1 Timothy 4:7)

For physical training is of some value, but godliness has value for all things, holding promise for both the present life and the life to come. (1 Timothy 4:8)

His divine power has given us everything we need for life and godliness through our knowledge of him who called us by his own glory and goodness. (2 Peter 1:3)

But just as he who called you is holy, so be holy

in all you do; for it is written: "Be holy, because I am holy." (1 Peter 1:15–16)

Do not be yoked together with unbelievers. For what do righteousness and wickedness have in common? Or what fellowship can light have with darkness? What harmony is there between Christ and Belial? What does a believer have in common with an unbeliever? What agreement is there between the temple of God and idols? For we are the temple of the living God. As God has said: "I will live with them and walk among them, and I will be their God, and they will be my people." "Therefore come out from them and be separate,/ says the Lord./ Touch no unclean thing,/ and I will receive you."/ "I will be a Father to you,/ and you will be my sons and daughters,/ says the Lord Almighty." (2 Corinthians 6:14–18)

Dear children, keep yourselves from idols. (1 John 5:21)

While by no means an exhaustive list, the above citation of passages may be taken as fairly representative of the teaching of the New Testament Scriptures on the subject of holiness.

IV. The two-fold aspect of holiness.

Holiness in the New Testament is presented under a

two-fold aspect, which may be called the *historical* and the *experimental*.

First, the Historical Aspect.

The sanctification of believers is represented as having been accomplished by Christ on the cross. Our holiness is part of the finished work of redemption. This aspect of the subject is sometimes called judicial or positional holiness. It has no reference whatever to the *character or state* of the believer, but rather to his *standing before God*. The citation of a few passages already quoted in another connection will make this phase of holiness clear:

> And by that will, we have been made holy through the sacrifice of the body of Jesus Christ once for all. (Hebrews 10:10)

> Because by one sacrifice he has made perfect forever those who are being made holy. (Hebrews 10:14)

> And so Jesus also suffered outside the city gate to make the people holy through his own blood. (Hebrews 13:12)

> To the church of God at Corinth, to those sanctified in Christ Jesus and called to be holy. (1 Corinthians 1:2a)

Second, The Experimental Aspect.

The sanctification of believers is also represented in the New Testament as an experimental possession, a present fact wrought out in the heart and life by the indwelling of the Holy Spirit. This aspect of holiness has no reference whatever to the believer's *standing before God,* but rather to his *character and state.* It means moral holiness, as we have come to understand the term. This is the more usual and familiar sense of sanctification and the one to which the great majority of passages that have been quoted refer. For example:

> But now that you have been set free from sin and have become slaves to God, the benefit you reap leads to holiness, and the result is eternal life. (Romans 6:22)

> May God himself, the God of peace, sanctify you through and through. May your whole spirit, soul and body be kept blameless at the coming of our Lord Jesus Christ. (1 Thessalonians 5:23)

> Make every effort to live in peace with all men and to be holy; without holiness no one will see the Lord. (Hebrews 12:14)

Now, these two phases of sanctification are distinct, yet vitally and inseparably connected. They are like the two halves that make a whole. What Christ did *for* us on the cross, the Spirit must do *in* us as a personal experience. The teaching of the Holy Scriptures is clear and emphatic that the believer's *state in grace* must conform to his *standing before God*. One passage will suffice:

> Since we have these promises, dear friends, let us purify ourselves from everything that contaminates body and spirit, perfecting holiness out of reverence for God. (2 Corinthians 7:1)

The attempt to divorce judicial holiness from experimental holiness is always attended by consequences more or less disastrous to moral character and conduct. Of sanctification as well as of marriage it is true, "What God hath joined together, let no man put asunder." There are Christians who think that judicial holiness is sufficient, and who make their sanctification by the cross an excuse and a justification for an unsanctified life. They feel that since their standing before God is perfect, it matters little if their walk before men is imperfect.

Then there are other Christians who do not go quite so far, yet who are unconcerned over irregularities in their character and conduct unbecoming the children of God. By some it would even seem as if Christ's work of sanctification on the cross was believed to grant a certain degree of moral laxity. Evidently, such Christians are guilty of sin, according to the plain teaching of the Scriptures; yet they rarely admit that they are guilty. Not infrequently, indeed, they condone their faults, seeming at times almost to extol them into virtues. What the Bible calls sin, these believers call "mistakes" or "infirmities." But of course all this is entirely wrong, being not only contrary to Scripture but also destructive of moral sense.

In discussing this very subject of the relation of the Christian to the law, Paul asks: "What shall we say then? Shall we go on sinning so that grace may increase? By no means! We died to sin; how can we live in it any longer?" (Romans 6:1–2). It is indeed, this belief, and worse still, this kind of Christian life that turns away so many people who are really spiritually hungry from the otherwise attractive doctrine of scriptural holiness. Such a profession is a distortion and a perversion of the truth. Judicial sanctification alone does not save from the power of sin and the tyranny of the flesh. Those believers who possess nothing more than historical holiness are in reality the bondservants of sin, and are "of all men most miserable."

V. The *Mode* of Holiness.

We come, finally, to consider the mode or process of holiness as set forth in the New Testament. Just as in the Old Testament, this by *contact with God.* If the contact is external or material, the holiness is ceremonial. But if, on the other hand, the contact is internal or spiritual, the holiness is moral. And if the contact with God is in any wise broken, holiness is lost. For, *holiness is retained only while contact with God is maintained.*

First, Ceremonial Holiness
Very little, comparatively, is said in the New Testament about ceremonial holiness. Dispensationally, the

Levitical offerings and ritual cleansing belong to the Old Testament. These things were a type of Christ. They were the *shadow* of which He is the *substance*, and they were all done away with in Him (Colossians 2:17; Hebrews 8:5; 10:1).

Yet the Jews in Christ's day observed, to a more or less extent, the Mosaic ceremonial system. Indeed, in His clashes with the Pharisees, Jesus condemned them, because they regarded ceremonial holiness as all that God required (Matthew 5:29; 6:16; 23:13–33; Mark 7:1–23; Luke 6:37–54). When Jesus healed the lepers, He commanded them to observe the ritual cleansing enjoined by the law (Matthew 8:4; Luke 17:14). The enemies of Christ would not enter Pilate's judgment hall, lest they should be defiled and thus made unfit to eat the passover (John 18:28). Pilate himself washed his hands as a symbol that he was innocent of the blood of Jesus (Matthew 27:24). The Apostle Paul on one occasion was under the vow of a Nazarite (Acts 18:18; Numbers 6:18). We further read of Paul and four men, who on the advice of James and in order to allay the prejudice of the Jews, purified themselves, and entering into the temple, made the offerings prescribed by the law (Acts 21:20–26).

As further examples of the mode of ceremonial holiness let us take two passages already quoted in another connection.

The first instance is First Corinthians 7:14. It is the case of an unbeliever being married to a believer and becoming "sanctified" by the holy life of the partner. Here the marriage tie is the means whereby the one who is not a Christian is accounted holy. In the same way a sanctifying influence is extended to the children of such a union. This does not, of course, mean that the children are saved; they still have need of the new birth. But they are covered by a Christian home, and by the faith of one of the parents are brought under the protection of the covenant mercies of God.

The second instance is First Timothy 4:4–5. Here the Jewish law concerning the distinction between clean and unclean animals is in question. This distinction was originally made to help the Israelites to understand the difference between moral defilement and moral holiness. (See Leviticus, chapter 11). The Jews extended the distinction to human life, regarding the people of all other nations as unclean.

It was this view that led Peter, upon being sent for, to hesitate to go to Cornelius. But by the vision of a sheet let down from heaven filled with all manner of beasts and creeping things and fowls, the Lord showed him that under the gospel this old distinction in the animal world was done away with, and that now the Gentiles as well as the Jews were accounted clean in His sight. Peter learned his lesson, for in his message to Cornelius he said: "I now realize how true it is that God does not show favoritism but accepts men from every nation who fear him and do what is right" (Acts 10:34–35).

With reference to the animal world, and especially to food offered in sacrifice to idols, Paul states in Romans 14:14: "As one who is in the Lord Jesus, I am fully convinced that no food is unclean in itself. But if anyone regards something as unclean, then for him it is unclean." Whether, therefore, in the passage we are examining, the meat had been offered in sacrifice to idols or not, made no difference to the believer whose mind and heart were spiritually enlightened. "For everything God created is good, and nothing is to be rejected if it is received with thanksgiving" (1 Timothy 4:4). Here the means whereby the "creature of God" was sanctified was *"the Word of God and prayer."*

Second, Moral Holiness.

In connection with the mode of moral holiness in the Old Testament reference has already been made to the mystery attending all the operations of God, especially the working of divine grace in the human heart. Just how God does anything man may never fully understand. If we could always comprehend God, He would cease to be God. Nevertheless, the teaching of the New Testament, as well as that of the Old Testament, is clear that the holiness of man flows from *contact with God.* And this contact is established and maintained in a five-fold way: by the will of God, by the work of Christ, by the indwelling of the Spirit, by the faith of the believer, and by the Word of God. Let us look a little at each of these points.

1. Christians are sanctified by the will of God.

This is the *ground* of holiness.

> It is God's will that you should be sanctified: that you should avoid sexual immorality (1 Thessalonians 4:3).

Then he said, "Here I am, I have come to do
your will." He sets aside the first to establish the
second. And by that will, we have been made
holy through the sacrifice of the body of Jesus
Christ once for all. (Hebrews 10:9–10)

2. Again, Christians are sanctified by the work of Christ.

This is the *procuring cause* of holiness. It is the historical or judicial aspect of sanctification, which has
already been explained, and which perhaps, needs no
further consideration.

> Because by one sacrifice he has made perfect
> forever those who are being made holy.
> (Hebrews 10:14)

> And so Jesus also suffered outside the city gate to
> make the people holy through his own blood.
> (Hebrews 13:12)

3. Again, Christians are sanctified by the indwelling of the Holy Spirit.

The Holy Spirit is the *Agent*, so to speak, of our
holiness. On the divine side He is the connecting link
between God and the believer. This is, in part, the experimental aspect of sanctification elsewhere unfolded.

> And that is what some of you were. But you were
> washed, you were sanctified, you were justified in
> the name of the Lord Jesus Christ and by the
> Spirit of our God. (1 Corinthians 6:11)

But we ought always to thank God for you, brothers loved by the Lord, because from the beginning God chose you to be saved through the sanctifying work of the Spirit and through belief in the truth. (2 Thessalonians 2:13)

Who have been chosen according to the foreknowledge of God the Father, through the sanctifying work of the Spirit, for obedience to Jesus Christ and sprinkling by his blood. (1 Peter 1:2)

Thus sanctification is a divine work. It is ascribed to the joint action of the Trinity.

(a.) The Father sanctifies. "May God himself, the God of peace, sanctify you through and through. May your whole spirit, soul and body be kept blameless at the coming of our Lord Jesus Christ" (1 Thessalonians 5:23).

(b.) The Son sanctifies. "But if we walk in the light, as he is in the light, we have fellowship with one another, and the blood of Jesus, his Son, purifies us from all sin" (1 John 1:7).

(c.) The Holy Spirit sanctifies. "Who have been chosen according to the foreknowledge of God the Father, through the sanctifying work of the Spirit, for obedience to Jesus Christ and sprinkling by his blood" (1 Peter 1:2).

4. Again, Christians are sanctified by faith.

Faith is the human means of holiness. This is also, in part, the experimental aspect of sanctification. On the human side faith is the connecting link that brings the believer into vital *contact with God.*

> God, who knows the heart, showed that he accepted them by giving the Holy Spirit to them, just as he did to us. He made no distinction between us and them, for he purified their hearts by faith. (Acts 15:8–9)

> To open their eyes and turn them from darkness to light, and from the power of Satan to God, so that they may receive forgiveness of sins and a place among those who are sanctified by faith in me. (Acts 26:18)

> But we ought always to thank God for you, brothers loved by the Lord, because from the beginning God chose you to be saved through the sanctifying work of the Spirit and through belief in the truth. (2 Thessalonians 2:13)

5. Finally, Christians are sanctified by the Word of God.

The Holy Scriptures, in connection with the divine Spirit and the faith of the believer, complete the means whereby experimental sanctification is secured.

> Sanctify them by the truth; your word is truth. (John 17:17)

Here the expression "word is truth" probably refers both to the Incarnate Word and the Written Word.

> Husbands, love your wives, just as Christ loved the church and gave himself up for her to make her holy, cleansing her by the washing with water through the word. (Ephesians 5:25–26)

> You are already clean because of the word I have spoken to you. (John 15:3)

While sanctification is a divine work, there is one sense in which the child of God may be said to sanctify himself. This is by the use of the Scriptures, illuminated by the Holy Spirit. In this light we are to understand a class of passages, of which the exhortation in Second Corinthians 7:1 is a striking example: "Since we have these promises, dear friends, let us purify ourselves from everything that contaminates body and spirit, perfecting holiness out of reverence for God." (See also Colossians 3:8–9; Hebrews 10:22; James 1:21; 1 Peter 2:2.) In this connection we may also notice Psalm 119:9: "How can a young man keep his way pure?/ By living according to your word."

Now, it is only through the Holy Scriptures that the child of God can cleanse himself from all filthiness of the flesh and spirit. How, then, is this cleansing accomplished? By the joint action of the Word of God and the Spirit of Truth applying the blood of Christ to the heart and life. Among the emblems of the Scriptures are the mirror and the laver.

First, the Bible is a mirror of revelation. It shows us our need of cleansing.

> Do not merely listen to the word, and so deceive yourselves. Do what it says. Anyone who listens to the word but does not do what it says is like a man who looks at his face in a mirror and, after looking at himself, goes away and immediately forgets what he looks like. But the man who looks intently into the perfect law that gives freedom, and continues to do this, not forgetting what he has heard, but doing it—he will be blessed in what he does. (James 1:22–25)

Second, the Bible is a laver of cleansing. What the light of truth reveals, the blood of Christ cleanses.

> Husbands, love your wives, just as Christ loved the church and gave himself up for her to make her holy, cleansing her by the washing with water through the word. (Ephesians 5:25–26) (See also Exodus 30:17–21; John 15:3; and Titus 3:5).

When the believer comes to the Scriptures with his mind and heart illuminated by the Holy Ghost, he finds his condition of life portrayed therein. Just as a mirror reflects dirt on the face, so the Bible is a mirror of revelation, not only disclosing crooked ways but also uncovering secret faults. Indeed, to make use of another Scriptural figure, the Word of God is "living and active. Sharper than any double-edged sword, it penetrates even to dividing soul and spirit, joints and marrow; it judges the thoughts and attitudes of the heart" (Hebrews 4:12). The Holy Ghost comes with the light of truth in one hand, so to speak, and the blood of Christ in the other. *What the light reveals, the blood cleanses.* This is the meaning of 1 John 1:7.

> But if we walk in the light, as he is in the light, we have fellowship with one another, and the blood of Jesus, his Son, purifies us from all sin.

Here the Greek verb translated "purifies" is in the present tense, indicative mood, and its force is to express *continuous action in present time.* Literally, as already mentioned, it may be rendered "keeps purifying," or, even better, "keeps on purifying." The idea is this: if we keep walking (here the verb is in the present subjunctive, denoting continuous action, too) in the light, the blood will keep purifying us: and the result will be that we shall have fellowship with one another. That is, primarily, the child of God will have fellowship with the Father; and secondarily, the children of God will have fellowship with one another.

Thus, there is a cleansing power in the Word of God, when applied to our hearts by the divine Spirit. How often the blessed Comforter brings a passage of Scripture or a personal message to our souls with purifying influence! May this indeed not have been what the Psalmist had in mind, when he prayed: "You know my folly, O God; my guilt is not hidden from you" (Psalm 69:5).

Now, in conclusion, let us briefly review the ground we have covered in our study of Scriptural holiness, emphasizing some already familiar facts and anticipating, perhaps, some new points yet to be more fully developed.

1. In a general way it may be said that the scriptural words for holiness or sanctification have three meanings, namely: first, separation from sin; second, dedication to God; and third, appointment to ministry. The fundamental idea is *the setting apart of a person or thing for the work of God.*

2. Holiness is of two kinds—ceremonial and moral. Ceremonial holiness belongs alike to persons and things. Moral holiness belongs only to persons. Ceremonial or official holiness is purely a matter of external relationship to God, and invests a person or thing with a sense of *sacredness.* Moral holiness, as the term implies, is spiritual renovation of character and practical righteousness of conduct.

3. As a divine attribute holiness is *purity.* God is pure from every thought, feeling and deed of evil.

4. Likewise, as a requirement of the Christian holiness is *purity.* The child of God, like his Father, must be free from every thought, feeling and deed of evil. Purity is not merely a negative quality, but a positive attribute as well. Both in God Himself and in the child of God purity involves the possession of righteousness, goodness and truth. In a word, the

believer must have the holiness of renewed character and of righteous conduct.

> For it is written: "Be holy, because I am holy." (1 Peter 1:16)

5. The holiness of the Christian is the holiness of Christ. All that God the Father is and all that He requires of His children, He has embodied in His Son. "For in Christ all the fullness of the Deity lives in bodily form, and you have been given fullness in Christ, who is the head over every power and authority" (Colossians 2:9–10).

As we cannot offer to God a holiness of our own, He offers to us a holiness of His own. Nor is the Giver apart from the gift; "Both the one who makes men holy and those who are made holy are of the same family. So Jesus is not ashamed to call them brothers" (Hebrews 2:11).

The holiness that God offers to us is the holiness of His Son. Christ is the sum and substance of the believer's sanctification. In fact, every instance of the use of the word holiness or sanctification in the Scriptures seems to be connected, whether typically or vitally, with the person of the Lord. Indeed, in one passage at least this inseparable connection between holiness and the Holy One becomes actual identification. "It is because of him that you are in Christ Jesus, who has become for us wisdom from God—that is, our righteousness, holiness and redemption" (1 Corinthians 1:30).

6. Our holiness flows from contact with God. This contact has both a divine and a human side. On the divine side there are two points of contact—the work of Christ on the cross, and the personal indwelling of the Holy Ghost. On the human side there are likewise two points of contact, whereby we become partakers of the holiness of Christ—a step of entire surrender and an act of appropriating faith.

7. The result of such contact with Christ is a new Christian experience, a second definite work of grace—a crisis as radical and revolutionary as the crisis of conversion. In nature it is not a gradual development, but a sudden change. In regeneration we pass out of death into life; in sanctification we pass out of the self-life into the Christ-life. In regeneration we receive a "new spirit"; in sanctification the Holy Spirit definitely and personally comes and takes up His abode within the "new spirit." This second and distinct work of sanctification is connected with the definite and personal coming of the Holy Ghost to our hearts. After conversion the Holy Spirit is *with* us; but after sanctification the Holy Spirit is *within* us. To make use of the figure of another, in regeneration the Holy Spirit *builds* His temple; but in sanctification He moves in and *occupies* it. Thus, it is by the definite reception by faith of the person of the Holy Ghost that the vision of the indwelling Christ is made real to our hearts.

8. Sanctification means a radical and revolutionary transformation of personality—a clean life and a

blameless walk. But this renovation of character and conduct is only in and through Christ Himself. Apart from the person of the Sanctifier the blessing of sanctification would not be permanent. The cleansed temple must be possessed and occupied by the Lord of the temple. While the diver is connected with the atmosphere by the breathing tube, he has all the air he needs; but disconnect the breathing tube and the diver dies. Put an iron in among the coals, and the iron is in the fire and the fire is in the iron, and while the iron is among the coals, the fire extends to and sets in rapid motion every particle of the iron; but take the iron out of the fire, and it grows cold and the particles become still. In like manner, while a believer is in vital contact of conscious fellowship with Christ, the holiness of Christ flows into the believer and becomes his personal possession, transforming his character and conduct. But apart from Christ, the believer becomes cold and dead. Therefore, by loving obedience and living fellowship we must abide in Christ; for, as Jesus said, "apart from me you can do nothing" (John 15:6).

The Vision of Victory

In mountain climbing it is a good thing to rest occasionally and look back over the land that lies below and try to catch a glimpse of the height that looms beyond. So in our ascent of the pathway to victory let us pause now for a review and an outlook.

At the outset we saw that Christianity is inseparable from the person of Christ; that He is the sum of all the doctrines of grace and the substance of all the fruit of the Spirit. Then we saw that salvation begins in deliverance from the penalty and guilt of sin and in receiving a new heart and a new spirit. Next we saw that after the birth from above comes the wilderness experience with its ceaseless struggle and inevitable defeat. Inquiring diligently for the cause of this mixed experience, we saw that it was the poison of sin. And finally, having seen what sin is, we found the antidote to be divine holiness.

This is the review. What, now, is the outlook? Well, it is one thing to diagnose a disease and analyze the properties of its specific remedy. It is quite another thing, however, to apply the remedy and cure the disease. In other words, it is one thing to know what sin is and understand the teaching of the Scriptures concerning holiness. But it is quite another thing to conquer sin and enter upon a life of practical victory. We have seen the need and nature of sanctification: this is the land that lies below. All along, however, we have been catching occasional glimpses of the "higher ground."

We have seen that the holiness of the Christian flows from vital *contact with God.* This contact has both a divine and a human side. On the divine side there are two points of contact, namely: the cross of Christ, and the work of the Spirit.

The first point of divine contact, whereby holiness is received, is the cross of Christ; and the first step in the pathway of victory is a vision of the cross.

Vision precedes victory

In Christian experience the apprehension of divine truth comes before its appropriation and realization. Vision precedes victory. The child of God must see his spiritual inheritance before he can enter upon its actual possession. In sanctification the highlands of deliverance loom up while the believer is struggling along on the lowlands of defeat. It was this way in the typical history of the Israelites. While they were making their weary and dreary marches in the wilderness of Sinai, spies were sent over into Canaan. Twelve chosen men walked to and fro throughout the Land of Promise and brought back the grapes of Eschol as a sample of the fruitfulness of Jehovah. It was this way with the man in the seventh chapter of Romans. The star of hope appeared in the midnight of despair. It was while he was struggling for deliverance from the dominion of sin that his eye caught by faith a vision of the cross with its promise and potency of victory. Triumphantly, he shouted, "I thank God through Jesus Christ our Lord."

This shout of triumph gives us the keynote of deliverance. Let us try to see more clearly just what the vision of victory is. It is all wrapped up in the simple phrase: "through Jesus Christ our Lord." This expression means three things: First, our identification with Christ in His crucifixion; second, our identification with Christ in His resurrection; and third, Christ's identification with us through His personal indwelling.

I. Our identification with Christ in His crucifixion.

There are two aspects in which the believer stands related to the cross of Christ: *substitution* and *identification.*

Of these truths perhaps substitution is the more familiar. Christ died for us. He bore our sins on the cross. He took our place under wrath and endured the penalty that we deserved. This is the vision of the cross that comes to the helpless sinner; and when he appropriates it by faith it brings salvation from the guilt of sin. This is the meaning of "Christ our Savior." This substitutional aspect of the cross is typified in the Old Testament by the scapegoat in the

16th chapter of Leviticus. Aaron laid both his hands upon the head of the scapegoat and confessed over it all the iniquities of the children of Israel. In symbol all the transgressions of the people were put upon the head of the goat, which was afterwards led away into the wilderness to die. It was regarded as an unclean thing and its whole body was counted a mass of corruption. This was the picture that Isaiah had in mind when he exclaimed:

> We all, like sheep, have gone astray, each of us has turned to his own way; and the Lord has laid on him the iniquity of us all. (Isaiah 53:6)

> And so Jesus also suffered outside the city gate to make the people holy through his own blood. (Hebrews 13:12)

The second aspect of our relation to the cross—identification—needs special emphasis, because it is not well understood by all Christians. Christ died for us—that is true; but it is only half the truth. We died in Christ—that is the other half of the truth. The statement is only partially true that Christ died for us that we might escape punishment. It requires also to be said that God regards us as having been punished in Christ. To make the truth more individual, in the person of my Substitute I bore the penalty of sin. In Him the law exhausted its power of death upon me. When Christ died, I died, too. With reference to the claim of the law and power of sin, I am, in the sight of God, counted as a dead man. This is what Paul meant, when he declared, "I have been crucified with Christ" (Galatians 2:20a). This also is the clear teaching of such passages as the following:

> We were therefore buried with him through baptism into death in order that, just as Christ was raised from the dead through the glory of the Father, we too may live a new life. If we have been united with him like this in his death, we will certainly also be united with him in his resurrection. (Romans 6:4–5)

> Because anyone who has died has been freed from sin. Now if we died with Christ, we believe that we will also live with him. (Romans 6:7–8)

> In the same way, count yourselves dead to sin but alive to God in Christ Jesus. (Romans 6:11)

> So, my brothers, you also died to the law through the body of Christ, that you might belong to another, to him who was raised from the dead, in order that we might bear fruit to God. (Romans 7:4)

> For Christ's love compels us, because we are convinced that one died for all, and therefore all died. (2 Corinthians 5:14)

> For you died, and your life is now hidden with Christ in God. (Colossians 3:3)

> Having been buried with him in baptism and
> raised with him through your faith in the power
> of God, who raised him from the dead. (Colos-
> sians 2:12)

II. Our identification with Christ in His resurrection.

This is the second part of the vision of victory. In
the same two aspects in which the believer stands related to the crucifixion of Christ he also stands related
to His resurrection—substitution and identification.
Christ was our Substitute both in His crucifixion and
in His resurrection. Not only did He die for us on the
cross, but for us also He arose from the grave.

> He was delivered over to death for our sins and
> was raised to life for our justification. (Romans
> 4:25)

> And if Christ has not been raised, our preaching
> is useless and so is your faith. And if Christ has
> not been raised, your faith is futile; you are still
> in your sins. But Christ has indeed been raised
> from the dead, the firstfruits of those who have
> fallen asleep. (1 Corinthians 15:14, 17, 20)

Thus, the death of Christ alone would not have
saved; His resurrection was necessary to complete our
redemption.

Now, in His resurrection, as well as in His
crucifixion, the believer is identified with Christ. This

is what Paul meant when he said, "I have been crucified with Christ and I no longer live, but Christ lives in me" (Galatians 2:20a). To make the truth personal, I died with Christ, but I also rose with Him. I was in Him when He hung on the cross and when He lay in the grave, but I was also in Him when He burst the bands of death on the morning of the resurrection. Indeed, the Apostle Paul carries the identification still farther: "[God] made us alive with Christ even when we were dead in transgressions—it is by grace you have been saved. And God raised us up with Christ and seated us with him in the heavenly realms in Christ Jesus" (Ephesians 2:5–6). "Crucified with Christ"—this expresses the death-side of our union with the Lord. "Raised up with Christ"—this expresses the life-side of our union with Him. Let us take a few verses which bring out this life-side of our union with Christ—our identification with Him in His resurrection:

> We were therefore buried with him through baptism into death in order that, just as Christ was raised from the dead through the glory of the Father, we too may live a new life. (Romans 6:4)

> In the same way, count yourselves dead to sin but alive to God in Christ Jesus. (Romans 6:11)

> For Christ's love compels us, because we are convinced that one died for all, and therefore all died. And he died for all, that those who live should no longer live for themselves but for him

who died for them and was raised again. (2
Corinthians 5:14–15)

Having been buried with him in baptism and
raised with him through your faith in the power
of God, who raised him from the dead. (Colossians 2:12)

Since, then, you have been raised with Christ, set
your hearts on things above, where Christ is
seated at the right hand of God. For you died,
and your life is now hidden with Christ in God.
(Colossians 3:1, 3)

III. Christ's identification with us through His personal indwelling.

This is the last part of the vision of victory and the
most glorious of all. Christ Himself by the Holy
Spirit, will come and dwell in our hearts and live out
His own life within us. This is what Paul meant, when
he said, "I have been crucified with Christ and I no
longer live, but Christ lives in me" (Galatians 2:20a).
This also is the clear teaching of such passages as the
following:

On that day you will realize that I am in my
Father, and you are in me, and I am in you.
Whoever has my commands and obeys them, he
is the one who love me. He who loves me will be
loved by my Father, and I too will love him and
show myself to him. (John 14:20–21)

> To them God has chosen to make known among the Gentiles the glorious riches of this mystery, which is Christ in you, the hope of glory. (Colossians 1:27)

It is a glorious revelation that Christ will live in us and manifest Himself to us. Can we take in this sublime truth with its stupendous significance? The Christ who was born as a babe in Bethlehem; who grew to manhood in the humble home in Nazareth; who lived a life of holy obedience to His Father's will; who died on the cross as a sacrifice for sin; who ascended to heaven and seated Himself at the right hand of God as our Advocate and High Priest; and who is coming back again to this dark and sin-cursed earth to transform it into Edenic beauty and reign in righteousness and peace:—this blessed Christ of God will come into my poor heart and make His home there and live out His own life within me by the indwelling presence and power of the Holy Spirit. Surely this must be the "full measure of the blessing of Christ" (Romans 15:29), of which the great apostle to the Gentiles speaks.

This, then, is the first step in the pathway to victory. The Christian who is struggling with sin and helpless in defeat must come to see that in the thought of God he was identified with Christ in His crucifixion and in His resurrection. Indeed, the transaction on Calvary was as real as if the child of God had himself actually died and been restored to life. Paul declares that not merely a part of himself—"the carnal mind," "the flesh" or "the old man"—but rather the whole of himself, so to speak, had passed through the mysterious and mystical experience of the cross. He uses personal pronouns. Thus, of himself he says, "*I* have been crucified with Christ and no longer live, but Christ lives in *me*" (Galatians 2:20a). Likewise, of believers he asserts, "For *you* died, and *your* life is now hidden with Christ in God" (Colossians 3:3). Yet there is no loss of individuality. Personal identity and moral responsibility are not destroyed. Just as it is the same seed that corrupts in the ground, yet germinates in beauty and fruitfulness, so it is the same believer who is crucified with Christ, yet is also risen with Him, evermore to "live a new life" (Romans 6:4). Not to His own death and resurrection alone, but as well to the death and resurrection of His people in Him, our Lord applied the wonderful principle of corruption and germination in nature in these words:

> I tell you the truth, unless a kernel of wheat falls to the ground and dies, it remains only a single seed. But if it dies, it produces many seeds. The man who loves his life will lose it, while the man who hates his life in this world will keep it for eternal life. (John 12:24–25)

Thus, the crucifixion and resurrection of the believer with Christ are not the extinction of his individual existence, but rather its reproduction and multiplication. Moreover, the use of the personal pronoun marks the continuity of conscious life. Thus, "I have been crucified with Christ and I no longer live, but Christ lives in me" (Galatians 2:20a). Again,

"Now if we died with Christ, we believe that we will also live with him" (Romans 6:8).

But now, if the identification of the believer with Christ in crucifixion and resurrection does not involve the loss of individuality or the destruction of personal identity and moral responsibility, what does take place? Ah! Herein is one of the miracles and mysteries of redemption. The cross has a *separating power*. It separates us from the *world*, from our *sins*, from our *sin*, and from *self*. When by faith we identify ourselves with Christ in His death, we are released from "the carnal mind"; we are separated from "the flesh"; we are detached from the *self-life*. In short, we "put off [our] old self, which is being corrupted by its deceitful desires" (Ephesians 4:22).

But the cross has a power of attachment as well as a power of detachment. While it detaches us from the old life of nature, it attaches us to the new life of grace. When by faith we identify ourselves with Christ in His resurrection, we become "made new in the attitude of [our] minds"; we "put on the new self, created to be God in true righteousness and true holiness" (Ephesians 4:23–24); and, highest of all, we "clothe [ourselves] with the Lord Jesus Christ" (Romans 13:14), who is thus "[our] holiness" (1 Corinthians 1:30).

Thus, through the cross of Christ, God has made provision whereby, without the loss of individuality or the destruction of personal identity and moral responsibility, believers are *detached from the old life of the flesh, and attached to the new life of the Spirit*. "But he who unites himself with the Lord is one with him in spirit" (1 Corinthians 6:17). The cross destroys the dominion of sin and the power of the flesh. Self is dethroned, and Christ is enthroned. The process is indeed mysterious and mystical, but the result is very real and practical.

Far more sublime and glorious than either eradication or suppression is the truth of the indwelling Christ. Eradication would take out of the heart the principle of sin, while suppression would keep the principle of sin bound down and in subjection in the heart. But sanctification through the indwelling Christ means that not only the principle of sin, but the heart itself in which the principle of sin resides; yea more—the very person himself in his entire being is nailed to the cross and is raised again in vital and inseparable union with the Lord. So that we may now say with Paul, "I have been crucified with Christ and I no longer live, but Christ lives in me. The life I live in the body, I live by faith in the Son of God, who loved me and gave himself for me" (Galatians 2:20).

> Once there lived another man within me,
>   Child of earth and slave of Satan he;
> But I nailed him to the cross of Jesus,
>   And that man is nothing now to me.
>
> Now Another Man is living in me,
>   And I count His blessed life as mine;
> I have died with Him to all my own life;
>   I have ris'n to all His life divine.
> —*Rev. A.B. Simpson*

Baptism

Of this two-fold identification of the believer with Christ in His death and resurrection baptism is an impressive symbolical representation. The popular conception of the ordinance of baptism is that it is a sort of badge of Christianity. Just as a member of a lodge or fraternal order receives a badge or medal as evidence of his initiation, so baptism is regarded as a sign of membership in a Christian church. There is of course a measure of truth in this view, inasmuch as baptism is one of the marks of distinction between a believer and an unbeliever. But Christian baptism is the sign and seal of our *union* with Christ, and the Lord's Supper is a sign and seal of our *communion* with Christ.

Baptism has a two-fold significance. In the first place, it is the outward sign and visible seal of the inner work of grace wrought by the Spirit of God in regeneration. It is the testimony before the world of the fact of conversion. It is a personal confession of Jesus Christ as Savior and Lord and of the decision to follow His footsteps in holy obedience. The candidate is not only baptized into the name of the Father, the Son and the Holy Spirit, but he is made partaker of the divine nature. In the New Testament the rite of baptism is connected with the grace of forgiveness. Indeed, so close is this relationship that many mistake the outward ceremony for the inward experience. But while baptism and the forgiveness of sins go together, yet the remission of sins or regeneration comes first.

In fact, the rite of baptism presupposes that the one who is baptized has already been forgiven and been begotten from above. The relationship is similar to that between betrothal and marriage. The wedding ceremony presupposes that the two hearts have been made one by the plighted troth; otherwise, there is a wedding only in name. So, the ordinance of baptism apart from the vital union of the soul with Christ becomes a mere form.

But, in the second place, baptism in its deeper spiritual meaning is a symbol of death. It is not a rite of cleansing, but a type of crucifixion. Thus the Apostle Paul says:

> Or don't you know that all of us who were baptized into Christ Jesus were baptized into his death? We were therefore buried with him through baptism into death in order that, just as Christ was raised from the dead through the glory of the Father, we too may live a new life. (Romans 6:3–4)

> Having been buried with him in baptism and raised with him through your faith in the power of God, who raised him from the dead. (Colossians 2:12)

Thus, baptism is a symbolical representation of the believer's death, burial and resurrection with Christ. It is, as someone has graphically expressed it, "the funeral service of the old life."

On the one hand, we are "buried with Him through

baptism into death" and on the other hand, we are "raised with Him through your faith in the power of God," in order that "just as Christ was raised from the dead through the glory of the Father, we too live a new life."

Many Christians do not see this deeper meaning of baptism. Others, like the Roman disciples, come to see it subsequent to the administration of the ordinance. But some children of God see it and enter into it at the very time of their baptism. In fact, in many instances it is the desire to follow their Lord in holy obedience that leads believers to be baptized. It is, indeed, of the very highest importance to see that baptism means death and resurrection, since to the mind and heart that are thus spiritually illuminated, this fact becomes an aid to practical holiness. The believer who enters by faith, either at the time or at a later season, into the deeper significance of baptism is enabled thereby the better to realize experimentally the sanctifying power of the truth of his union with Christ in His death and resurrection.

Discouraged and despairing heart, this is the pathway to victory. Do you catch the vision? On that dark day of the crucifixion, nearly 2000 years ago, you died with your Lord on Calvary and with Him were laid away in Joseph's tomb. But on that bright and glorious morning of the resurrection you stepped forth with your Lord from the open grave, evermore to "walk in newness of life (KJV)." Beloved, do you not see the truth? Look! Like Moses on Nebo's lofty height the Land of Promise even now is spread out before your fainting eyes. It is true that Moses died outside the land; but it is your glorious privilege to enter in. If you have seen the vision, God will make it real. He does not mock His children with vain hopes. He does not, like the mirage of the desert, lure on the thirsting soul to disappointment and disaster. Your feet are yet to tread the Land of Promise. You are to enter into rest. You are to be set free from the law of sin and death by the law of the Spirit of life in Christ Jesus. But you must see your inheritance before you can possess it. Apprehension comes first, and then appropriation. The vision precedes the victory.

It cannot be too strongly emphasized that the Christian life is a Christ life. It is not an imitation, but an incarnation. We do not copy Christ, we reproduce Him; or, rather, He reproduces His own life within us by the indwelling of the Holy Spirit.

A young American student sat in a national art gallery in Europe trying to copy a famous painting by one of the old masters. Patiently he toiled at his easel, but with unsatisfactory results. His work was a poor imitation of the original. One day he fell asleep over his canvas and as he slept he dreamed. He dreamed that the spirit of the old master took possession of his brain and hand. Eagerly he seized his brush, and rapidly reproduced the masterpiece before him. His work received the highest praise. It had the artistic finish and touch of genius as the original. At once his picture took its place among the famous paintings of the world, and the young artist himself was acclaimed as a new master. But the poor student awoke to find it all a dream, and in bitter disappointment applied himself to his fruitless task.

But, beloved, spiritually the young artist's dream may be gloriously true. We study the character of Christ as portrayed in the gospels. We recognize that His spotless purity and perfect obedience constitute the only standard of character and conduct acceptable to God. Then we try to imitate Christ. We struggle for His spotless purity and strive after His perfect obedience. But at every turn we fail. Finally, in our discouragement and despair, God gives us the vision of the indwelling Christ. The divine Master will live in His disciples. Inseparably He will unite Himself to us, blending His life with ours and our lives with His. Christ will think through our minds. Christ will love through our hearts. Christ will act through our wills. Christ will keep the law within us. Christ will please His Father within us. Christ will destroy the dominion of sin and the power of the flesh, dethrone self, and reign supreme in our lives. In a word, all we cannot be and all we cannot do of ourselves Christ Himself will be within us and do within us. May we make these lines from a poem by Frances Ridley Havergal our prayer:

> Live out Thy life within me,
>   O Jesus, King of kings;
> Be Thou Thyself the answer
>   To all my questionings.

CHAPTER

8

The Realization of Victory

There remaineth therefore a rest to the people of God" (Hebrews 4:9, KJV). This is not the rest of reward in heaven, but the rest of faith here upon earth. It is a triumphant Christian life, an experience of relief from struggle, of deliverance from sin, and of victory over self through the indwelling of the risen Christ and the baptism and fullness of the Holy Spirit. Not for realization but for inspiration are the ideals of common life, but in spiritual life visions may become verities. Thus after the vision of victory comes the realization of victory. What the believer has apprehended by divine illumination he must also appropriate by an act of entire surrender and a step of aggressive faith.

The vision of victory apart from its realization is powerless to deliver. From Mount Nebo's lofty height Moses viewed the landscape of Canaan, but he died outside in the barren wastes of Moab. The children of Israel caught a glimpse of Canaan through the report of the spies, but they perished in the weary and dreary wilderness. Moses was kept out of the Land of Promise by disobedience and the Israelites could not enter in because of their unbelief (Hebrews 3:19). Of the entire generation that left Egypt, Caleb and Joshua alone crossed the Jordan. They received their covenant inheritance because they "wholly followed the Lord."

Moreover, a vision without victory works harm to the soul. Loss always results from the apprehension of spiritual truth apart from its realization. Indeed, one can never see divine things and afterwards be quite the same. For this reason God sometimes withholds light that He knows will not be followed. If the heavenly light is permitted to fade away, the heart will be left in even greater darkness. If the vision of victory over the dominion of sin and the power of the flesh through the indwelling Christ is not transformed into a glorious reality by the definite reception of the gift of the Holy Spirit through a step of entire surrender and an act of appropriating faith, the believer will be plunged into struggles and defeats still more hopeless and despairing. We dare not, then, pause on the threshold of our inheritance. We have now put our hand to the plow, so to speak; to go back, or even to look back, would be to invite spiritual disaster. With reference to the deeper life of faith the writer of the epistle to the Hebrews says:

And if he shrinks back,
I will not be pleased with him.

By way of encouragement, however, he quickly adds:

But we are not of those who shrink back and are destroyed, but of those who believe and are saved. (Hebrews 10:38–39)

How, then, may the vision of victory be transformed into the realization of victory? *By the definite reception of the gift of the Holy Spirit through a step of entire surrender and an act of appropriating faith.* We have already seen that the holiness of the Christian flows from *contact with God.* This contact has both a divine and human side. On the divine side there are two points of contact, namely: the identification of the believer with Christ in His death and resurrection and the definite reception of the gift of the Holy Spirit. On the human side there are also two points of contact, namely: a step of entire surrender and the receiving of the Holy Spirit through an act of appropriating faith.

Now, the identification of the believer with Christ in His death and resurrection is the historical and incomplete side of holiness; the transformation of the believer in character and conduct through the reception of the gift of the Holy Spirit is the experimental and complete side of holiness. The vision of the cross and the indwelling Christ is the first step in the pathway to victory. That step we have already taken. The definite reception of the gift of the Holy Spirit through a step of entire surrender and an act of appropriating faith is the second step in the pathways to victory. This step we are now to take.

In regeneration God gives us a "new spirit." In sanctification He puts within us the Holy Spirit ("My

Spirit" Ezekiel 36:26–27). Regeneration is the result of the *gracious inworking* of the Holy Spirit. Sanctification is the result of the *personal indwelling* of the Holy Spirit. Consequently, after regeneration the Holy Spirit is *with* us; but after sanctification He is *within* us. Now, the experience of sanctification through the indwelling Christ is realized in connection with the definite reception of the gift of the Holy Spirit by full consecration and living faith. Indeed, it is through the Holy Spirit that we come to see the hopelessness of struggling against sin. It is through the Holy Spirit that we catch a glimpse of the cross with its promise and potency of deliverance. It is through the Holy Spirit that the revelation of the indwelling Christ breaks with comforting cheer upon our despairing hearts. It is through the Holy Spirit that we are enabled to die unto sin and live unto God.

First, the reception of the gift of the Holy Ghost

I. The Experience of the Apostolic Church.

In the experience of the Apostolic Church, as recorded in the book of Acts, there were three things that were closely connected, namely: conversion, baptism and the reception of the Holy Spirit. Thus on the day of Pentecost Peter declared:

> Repent and be baptized every one of you, in the name of Jesus Christ for the forgiveness of your sins. And you will receive the gift of the Holy

> Spirit. The promise is for you and your children and for all who are far off—for all whom the Lord our God will call. (Acts 2:38–39)

Now, in this passage of Scripture three facts would seem to be clear. First, conversion (here described as the forgiveness of sins) baptism, and the reception of the gift of the Holy Spirit, are three separate and distinct things. Second, these three things, while separate and distinct, are yet closely related both as doctrines and as experiences. And third, these three things are here stated in their normal order and scriptural relationship. When a sinner is converted he should seek baptism as the open confession of his faith in Christ as Savior and Lord, and as the sign and seal of his identification by faith with Christ in His death and resurrection. Then he should definitely receive the Holy Spirit, who by His indwelling and infilling will become the enabling for a life well pleasing to God and the equipping for a life of fruitful service to man.

The relation of the reception of the Holy Spirit to the experience of conversion in Acts is an interesting study. A careful examination of the book leads to two conclusions, namely: First, in some instances the Holy Spirit was received *at the time of* conversion; and second, in other instances the Holy Spirit was received *subsequent to* conversion.

1. In some instances the Holy Ghost was received at the time of conversion. This was the case on the Day of Pentecost and in the house of Cornelius.

From the language of Peter, already quoted (Acts 2:38–39), we learn that on the Day of Pentecost conversion, baptism and the reception of the Holy Ghost went together. That is, while these three things were separate and distinct experiences, yet no interval of time elapsed between conversion and baptism on the one hand, or between conversion and the reception of the Holy Spirit on the other.

> Those who accepted his message were baptized, and about three thousand were added to their number that day. (Acts 2:41)

The case of Cornelius and his household is recorded in Acts 10:44–48:

> While Peter was still speaking these words, the Holy Spirit came on all who heard the message. The circumsized believers who had come with Peter were astonished that the gift of the Holy Spirit had beeen poured out even on the Gentiles. For they heard them speaking in tongues and praising God.
>
> Then Peter said, "Can anyone keep these people from being baptized with water? They have received the Holy Spirit just as we have." So he ordered that they be baptized in the name of Jesus Christ. Then they asked Peter to stay with them for a few days.

Here also, as on the Day of Pentecost, conversion is connected with the reception of the Holy Spirit, although the two experiences were separate and distinct. On this occasion, it will be observed, the reception of the Holy Spirit *preceded* baptism.

2. In other instances the Holy Spirit was received subsequent to conversion. This was true of the Samaritan disciples and the Ephesian disciples.

The case of the Samaritan disciples is recorded in Acts 8:12–17:

> But when they believed Philip as he preached the good news of the kingdom of God and the name of Jesus Christ, they were baptized, both men and women. Simon himself believed and was baptized. And he followed Philip everywhere, astonished by the great signs and miracles he saw.
>
> When the apostles in Jerusalem heard that Samaria had accepted the word of God, they sent Peter and John to them. When they arrived, they prayed for them that they might receive the Holy Spirit, because the Holy Spirit had not yet come upon any of them; they had simply been baptized into the name of the Lord Jesus. Then Peter and John placed their hands on them, and they received the Holy Spirit.

Now, observe that under the preaching of Philip, the Samaritans "accepted the word of God." This is, they were converted or saved. Moreover, they received Christian baptism—"they had simply been baptized in the name of the Lord Jesus." But at a later date, or *subsequent to* their conversion, they received the Holy Spirit under the joint ministry of Peter and John. It is interesting to note that the Holy Spirit was given to the Samaritan disciples through prayer and the laying on of hands by the apostle.

The case of the Ephesian disciples is recorded in Acts 19:1–6:

> While Apollos was at Corinth, Paul took the road through the interior and arrived at Ephesus. There he found some disciples and asked them, "Did you receive the Holy Spirit when you believed?"
>
> They answered, "No, we have not even heard that there is a Holy Spirit."
>
> So Paul asked, "Then what baptism did you receive?"
>
> "John's baptism," they replied.
>
> Paul said, "John's baptism was a baptism of repentance. He told the people to believe in the one coming after him, that is, in Jesus." On hearing this, they were baptized into the name of the Lord Jesus. When Paul placed his hands on them, the Holy Spirit came on them, and they spoke in tongues and prophesied.

Paul's question in verse two, in the Revised Version, reads: "Did ye receive the Holy Ghost, when ye believed?" Now, whichever of these three renderings is preferred, four facts stand out clearly. First, the Ephesian disciples were Christians; yet at the time Paul met them, they had not received the Holy Spirit.

Second, conversion, therefore, and the reception of the Holy Spirit are separate and distinct experiences. Third, the Holy Spirit may be received at the time of conversion. And fourth, the Holy Spirit may be received subsequent to conversion. On this occasion, it will be observed, Christian baptism was administered some little time after conversion; and further, that the Holy Spirit was received in connection with Christian baptism and the laying on of hands by Paul.

The case of the Apostle Paul does not seem to be altogether clear. The record in Acts 9:17–18 reads:

> Then Ananias went to the house and entered it. Placing his hands on Saul, he said, "Brother Saul, the Lord—Jesus, who appeared to you on the road as you were coming here—has sent me so that you may see again and be filled with the Holy Spirit." Immediately, something like scales fell from Saul's eyes, and he could see again. He got up and was baptized.

Now, it does not appear to be altogether clear just at what time Paul was converted—whether on the road to Damascus, or during the three days of darkness. Consequently, there is an uncertainty as to whether the apostle received the Holy Spirit at the time of conversion, or subsequent thereto. In the latter event, the interval was very brief—amounting to only a few days. On this occasion, it will be observed, the Holy Spirit was received before Christian baptism.

Surely, from this brief study of the experience of the

Apostolic Church, as recorded in the book of Acts, we may learn that God is sovereign in His operation, and that doctrinal distinctions made by man cannot shut Him up to set ways of working. At the same time four things seem to be clear. First, conversion and the definite reception of the gift of the Holy Spirit are separate and distinct experiences. Second, conversion may occur without the experience of receiving the Holy Spirit. Third, the Holy Spirit is often received at the time of conversion. And fourth, the Holy Spirit is often received subsequent to conversion.

Now, in the light of these facts we believe that conversion and the reception of the Holy Spirit should go hand in hand, so to speak. That is, while they are distinct experimentally, they should not be separated chronologically. But in the lives of few Christians today, comparatively speaking, is this true. John Wesley tells of a man who was converted one hour, sanctified the second hour, and glorified the third hour. The man died three hours after he was saved. Indeed, where there is right scriptural teaching no interval of time need occur after conversion before the Holy Spirit is received. Unfortunately, however, this is seldom the case. Generally an interval of time—and often it is a long period—does occur. Indeed, some true hearted children of God never seem to know from experience the personal indwelling of the Holy Spirit. But this interval, where it occurs, is filled in with the weary marches and dreary experiences of the wilderness of Sinai, and with the ceaseless struggles and discouraging defeats of the seventh chapter of Romans. We cannot refrain from saying that we

believe God never intended that there should be a barren state of Christian experience between regeneration
and sanctification, but that conversion should be im-
mediately followed by a life of victory over sin and self
in union with the indwelling Christ and through
receiving the gift of the Holy Spirit.

II. The Teaching of the Apostolic Writings.

We have studied the experience of the Apostolic
Church, with reference to the definite reception of the
Holy Spirit, as recorded in the book of Acts. Now, let
us turn to the teaching of the epistles.

Let us cite a few passages which refer to the possession of the Holy Spirit or to the indwelling of the
risen Christ. These two classes of passages may be
grouped together, for it is the baptism of the Holy
Spirit which brings to our hearts the revelation of the
indwelling Christ.

> You, however, are controlled not by the sinful
> nature but by the Spirit, if the Spirit of God lives
> in you. And if anyone does not have the Spirit of
> Christ, he does not belong to Christ. But if
> Christ is in you, your body is dead because of
> sin, yet your spirit is alive because of righteous-
> ness. (Romans 8:9–10)

> Don't you know that you yourselves are God's
> temple and that God's Spirit lives in you? If
> anyone destroys God's temple, God will destroy

him; for God's temple is sacred, and you are that temple. (1 Corinthians 3:16–17)

For we were all baptized by one Spirit into one body—whether Jews or Greeks, slave or free—and we were all given the one Spirit to drink. (1 Corinthians 12:13)

Examine yourselves to see whether you are in the faith; test yourselves. Do you not realize that Christ Jesus is in you—unless, of course, you fail the test? (2 Corinthians 13:5)

I would like to learn just one thing from you: Did you receive the Spirit by observing the law, or by believing what you heard? (Galatians 3:2)

My dear children, for whom I am again in the pains of childbirth until Christ is formed in you. (Galatians 4:19)

For this reason I kneel before the Father, from whom his whole family in heaven and on earth derives its name. I pray that out of his glorious riches he may strengthen you with power through his Spirit in your inner being. So that Christ may dwell in your hearts through faith. And I pray that you, being rooted and established in love, may have power, together with all the saints, to grasp how wide and long and high and deep is the love of Christ, and to know this love that surpasses knowledge—that you may be filled to the measure of all fullness of God. (Ephesians 3:14–19)

To them God has chosen to make known among the Gentiles the glorious riches of this mystery, which is Christ in you, the hope of glory. (Colossians 1:27)

A careful examination of the above and similar passages discloses two striking facts. First, in some instances the baptism or possession of the Holy Spirit is closely identified with regeneration or conversion. Second, in other instances these experiences are separated in point of time. But this is just the conclusion that we reached from our study of the book of Acts. Thus the experience of the Apostolic Church and the teachings of the apostolic writings agree. And indeed, this must be so, for the Holy Spirit was the Inworker of the one as He was the Inspirer of the other. In fact, the words of Peter on the Day of Pentecost—Acts 2:38–39—give us the key, which explains the teaching of the New Testament on this vitally important theme. There we learn, as we have seen, that the remission of sins or conversion and the reception of the gift of the Holy Spirit, while closely related, are yet separate and distinct both doctrinally and experimentally. When this principle of interpretation is clearly understood and firmly grasped, two resulting facts will be readily admitted. First, the Holy Spirit may be received at the time of conversion; and second, the Holy Spirit may be receive subsequent to conversion.

III. The Spiritual Crisis of the Life of our Lord.

The baptism of our blessed Lord with the Holy Ghost was a spiritual crisis in His life. It marked alike the beginning of His encounters with Satan and the opening of His public ministry of teaching and healing. As a baby, Jesus was born in the Spirit in Bethlehem of Judea:

> The Holy Spirit will come upon you, and the power of the Most High will overshadow you. So the holy one to be born will be called the Son of God. (Luke 1:35)

Moreover, as a child and youth the Spirit of God was with Jesus of Nazareth. Luke gives us two exquisite pictures, one of boyhood and the other of the early manhood, of the Savior:

> And the child grew and became strong; he was filled with wisdom, and the grace of God was upon him.
> And Jesus grew in wisdom and stature, and in favor with God and men. (Luke 2:40, 52)

Thus, the life of Jesus, during the silent years of the home training in Nazareth, was the object of the Holy Spirit's special and peculiar care. The growth and symmetrical development of His spirit, mind and body were under the influence of the Holy Spirit that "the grace of God was upon Him," and that He "in-

creased in wisdom and stature, and in favor with God
and men." But at 30 years of age a marked crisis came
in the life of our Lord. It was then, at the river Jordan,
that Christ was not only baptized in water by John the
Baptist, but also baptized with the Holy Spirit by His
Heavenly Father. Here we read:

> When all the people were being baptized, Jesus
> was baptized too. And as he was praying, heaven
> was opened and the Holy Spirit descended on
> him in bodily form like a dove. And a voice came
> from heaven: "You are my Son, whom I love;
> with you I am well pleased." (Luke 3:21–22)

What, then, was the significance of this marked
crisis in the life of Christ? From His birth until His
baptism the Holy Spirit was *with* Christ; but from His
baptism until His passion the Holy Spirit was *within*
Him. After the crisis at the river Jordan two divine
personalities were inseparably united—Jesus of
Nazareth and the Spirit of God. From that hour the
life of Christ was wrought out in absolute dependence
upon the Holy Spirit. Thus it was through the Holy
Spirit that Christ met and overcame the devil in the
wilderness. It was through the Holy Spirit that Christ
uttered His matchless words and performed His
wondrous deeds. It was through the Holy Spirit that
Christ offered Himself as sacrifice on the cross. And it
was through the Holy Spirit that Christ was raised
from the dead and declared to be the Son of God with
power. The great difference, therefore, between the
private life and public ministry of Jesus Christ is ex-

plained by His baptism at the Jordan and the incoming and indwelling of the Holy Spirit.

Now, the Apostle John tells us that "in this world we are like him" (1 John 4:17). In this experience, therefore, as in all other things, Christ is our divine Pattern. So, after we have been born of the Spirit— and it should not be long afterwards—we must be baptized with the Spirit. It is then in connection with taking Christ as our sanctification that we receive the person of the Holy Spirit as our indwelling and abiding Comforter. When once He comes into our hearts, He never leaves us. We may indeed grieve Him, but we can never grieve Him away (Ephesians 4:30).

IV. The Significance of Typical Rites and Historical Incidents.

From the Scriptures as a whole let us gather up a few typical rites and historical incidents, the spiritual significance of which strengthens the conclusion that we have already reached, namely: that the reception of the Holy Ghost is an experience separate and distinct from conversion, but yet not necessarily far removed therefrom in point of time.

1. The crossing of the Jordan

As we have seen in chapter three, the passage of the Red Sea by the children of Israel was a type of regeneration, but the crossing of the Jordan was a type of sanctification. The Red Sea represented separation from the *world*, the Jordan represented separation from *self.* Both experiences symbolized *death* but the death symbolized by the Jordan was deeper than the death symbolized by the Red Sea. Before the conquering hosts could victoriously possess their inheritance in the land of Canaan Moses had to die, which represented our death to the *law*; the river Jordan had to be crossed, which represented our death to *sin*; the rite of circumcision had to be performed at Gilgal, which represented our death to the *flesh*; and Joshua had to surrender his own right of leadership and acknowledge the leadership of the "Captain of the Host of the Lord" which represented our death to *self.* Surely, all this is deeply significant of a second work of grace, a spiritual crisis after conversion, when by entire surrender and living faith we take the Holy Spirit to make real in us our identification with Christ in His death and resurrection and Christ's identification with us through His personal indwelling.

2. The Pillar of Cloud and Fire

From the passage of the Red Sea until the erection of the Tabernacle, the pillar of cloud and fire, the symbol of the Holy Spirit, went before the hosts of Israel, guiding them in the way and protecting them from peril. But after the Tabernacle was built, the pillar of cloud and fire, the emblem of God's personal presence, became the Shekinah glory, which rested over the mercy-seat and between the outstretched wings of the cherubim. No longer did God thunder His commands to Israel from Mount Sinai; but He "called to Moses and spoke to him from the Tent of Meetings [tabernacle of the congregation, KJV]" (Leviticus 1:1). Moreover, the time when this momentous change occurred is most suggestive. It was "the first day of the first month" of the second year, which marked a new epoch in the history of Israel.

Spiritually, the pillar of cloud and fire in advance of the marching hosts is typical of the *presence* of the Holy Spirit *with* us, as our Guide and Defender. But the hovering of the Shekinah glory over the mercy-seat and between the outstretched wings of the cherubim is typical of the *Person* of the Holy Spirit *within* us, as the Source of our holiness and the Spring of our service. Before we receive the Holy Spirit, He has to speak to us largely through the divine providence of our lives; but after we receive Him, He can speak to us more intimately by means of His personal presence in our hearts. Furthermore, the first day of the first month, of the second year, is suggestive of the new epoch in Christian experience which is marked by the personal incoming and indwelling of the Spirit of God.

3. The Blood and the Oil

In the ceremonial rites for the cleansing of the leper we have seen how he was first sprinkled seven times with the blood and then sprinkled seven times with the oil. The two rites were quite separate and distinct. The blood was a type of the redemption of Christ and the oil was a type of the baptism of the Holy Spirit. The oil was put upon the blood of the trespass offering. This order could not be changed. The cleansed leper could be anointed with oil only after he had been sprinkled with blood. Now, all this speaks to us

of salvation and sanctification. We must take Christ as
our Savior before we can receive the Holy Spirit.

4. The Promise of Christ

On one occasion Christ closed His instruction concerning prayer with these words: "If you then, though
you are evil, know how to give good gifts to your
children, *how much more will your Father in heaven
give the Holy Spirit to those who ask him?*" (Luke
11:13).

Here our Lord was addressing His followers, among
them manifestly being some who were saved; yet He
gives them the promise of the Holy Spirit, to be
received in answer to prayer.

Again, in the upper room, just before His betrayal,
the Master gave His disciples very explicit and definite
teaching concerning the Holy Spirit. One of His parting messages was:

> If you love me, you will obey what I command.
> And I will ask the Father, and he will give you
> another Counselor to be with you forever—the
> Spirit of truth. The world cannot accept him, be-
> cause it neither sees him nor knows him. But
> you know him, *for he lives with you and will be in
> you.* (John 14:15–17)

In verse 17 an important distinction is made in the
use of the prepositions "with" and "in." *With* is the
Greek *para*, and means "by the side of"; *in* is the
Greek *en*, and means "within." As we have seen there
is a vast difference between having the Holy Spirit

with us, and having Him *within* us. In the one case He is a presence *outside*, in the other case He is a Person *inside*. Plainly, the meaning is that before Pentecost the disciples had the Holy Spirit with them, but after Pentecost they were to have Him within them. This view of the Savior's words is supported by the discriminating way in which the tenses of the verbs are used. "Lives" is the present tense and refers to the time of Christ's speaking. "Will be" is the future tense and refers to a coming time. Evidently, the Day of Pentecost was in the mind of the Master.

Once again, after His resurrection, Christ referred very definitely to the approaching advent of the Holy Spirit:

> I am going to send you what my Father has promised; but stay in the city until you have been clothed with power from on high. (Luke 24:49)

> But you will receive power when the Holy Spirit comes on you; and you will be my witnesses in Jerusalem, and in all Judea and Samaria, and to the ends of the earth. (Acts 1:8)

Here the verse in Acts explains the passage in the Gospel of Luke. There is no *enduement of power* apart from the *incoming of the person*, and we know that on the Day of Pentecost the Person of the Holy Spirit, the Gift alike of the Father and of the Son, was received by the company of 120 disciples waiting in the upper room. The experience of these waiting disciples, therefore, teaches us the necessity of distinguishing between salvation by the blood of the crucified Christ and sanctification by the indwelling of the risen Christ. They were saved men and women, yet until they had received the Holy Spirit, they were not enabled for a life of holy obedience, nor equipped for a ministry of abiding fruitfulness. So today after the cleansing blood of the cross comes the enduing power of the upper room. Calvary is not sufficient; we must have our Pentecost.

Second, the two-fold condition of the reception of the gift of the Holy Spirit

Contact with God, whereby the Christian becomes partaker of the holiness of Christ, has a human as well as a divine side. On the human side contact is formed by a step of entire surrender and an act of appropriating faith. But these are the conditions of receiving the gift of the Holy Spirit. As such, therefore, we are now briefly to consider them.

I. A Step of Entire Surrender.

Another name for surrender is consecration. But as consecration is really a divine work, surrender is a better term. The Christian can yield his heart and life, but he cannot consecrate them; only God can do that. Thus, the Old Testament priests did not consecrate themselves. Moses, acting for Jehovah, consecrated them. The priests could only yield themselves to be consecrated (Leviticus 8:1–13; Romans 6:13; 7:1).

Surrender is giving up—a yielding to God. The believer must lay his whole life on the altar, relinquish all right to its control, and count himself henceforth and forever the Lord's. Surrender is a painful act. It means separation. It means sacrifice. It means self-denial. It means death. Before we come to know Christ as Savior we learn something of the meaning of surrender. It costs the sinner a good deal to give up the world with its pleasures and attractions. It is hard for him to separate himself from old associates and detach himself from old associations. But when we come to know Christ as our Sanctifier we learn the deeper meaning of surrender. It is one thing to give up the *world*; it is quite another thing to give up *oneself*. Yet this is what the Master requires of His disciples:

> If anyone would come after me, he must deny himself and take up his cross and follow me. (Matthew 16:24)

Now, self-denial, which is the essence of surrender, does not mean giving up *things*. It means giving up *self*. Self is securely seated upon the throne of the heart, and stubbornly refuses to abdicate in favor of Christ. But union with Christ means participation in His death. Now, in any form death is painful and terrible, at least in contemplation. It is perfectly natural that the self-life within us should shrink from the ordeal of crucifixion with Christ. Yet there is no escape therefrom, if we are ever to know the liberty and delight of a life of deliverance from the dominion of sin and from the tyranny of the flesh. Therefore, like our blessed Lord we must become "obedient to death—even death on a cross!" (Philippians 2:8). The self-life may shrink and quiver with pain. Yet we must take our place with the Lord on the cross and by a deliberate and determined act of the will hold ourselves there, while the Holy Spirit passes the iron of judgment and death through our souls.

Surrender to God must be voluntary, complete, and final.

1. It must be *voluntary.*

Unless the step of surrender is taken voluntarily, the surrender will be made only in name, and will have no spiritual value. God calls men and women, but does not coerce them. In making choices and in deciding destiny the will is free. It is true that God will supply motives to right action, but He will not arbitrarily determine the decision of the will. Accordingly, if the will does not yield, there is no surrender. And if the will is not free in its action, the surrender is not voluntary. Compulsory surrender is the result of force; voluntary surrender is the result of love.

In the Old Testament the type of voluntary surrender is the offering of Isaac on Mount Moriah. The angel of the Lord spoke thus to Abraham:

> I swear by myself, declares the Lord, that because you have done this and have not withheld your son, your only son, I will surely bless you. (Genesis 22:16–17a)

In the New Testament the example of voluntary surrender is the experience of Paul:

> But whatever was to my profit I now consider loss for the sake of Christ. What is more, I consider everything a loss compared to the surpassing greatness of knowing Christ Jesus my Lord, for whose sake I have lost all things. I consider them rubbish, that I may gain Christ and be found in him, not having a righteousness of my own that comes from the law, but that which is through faith in Christ—the righteousness that comes from God and is by faith. I want to know Christ and the power of his resurrection and the fellowship of sharing in his sufferings, becoming like him in his death, and so, somehow, to attain to the resurrection from the dead. (Philippians 3:7–11)

But higher than the offering of Isaac and the example of Paul is the spirit of voluntary surrender exhibited by our Lord, who is our divine Pattern.

> Sacrifice and offering you did not desire,
>   but my ears you have pierced;
> burnt offerings and sin offerings
>   you did not require.
> Then I said, "Here I am, I have come—
>   it is written about me in the scroll.
> I desire to do your will, O my God;
>   your law is within my heart."
>   (Psalm 40:6–8; see also Hebrews 10:5–9)

Your attitude should be the same as that of
  Christ Jesus:
Who, being in very nature God,
  did not consider equality with God something
    to be grasped,
but made himself nothing,
  taking the very nature of a servant,
  being made in human likeness.
And being found in appearance as a man,
  he humbled himself
  and became obedient to death—even death on
    a cross!
  (Philippians 2:5–8)

Therefore, I urge you, brothers, in view of God's
mercy, to offer your bodies as living sacrifices,
holy and pleasing to God—this is your spiritual
act of worship. Do not conform any longer to
the pattern of this world, but be transformed by
the renewing of your mind. Then you will be
able to test and approve what God's will is—his
good, pleasing and perfect will. (Romans 12:1–
2)

2. It must be *complete.*

Unless surrender be complete, it is not surrender at
all. A partial consecration is not sufficient; God will
not accept a divided heart. We must not keep back
part of the price. If we expect God to give Himself
wholly to us, we must give ourselves wholly to Him.

In the hour of surrender it is a good thing to make a mental inventory of our lives—spirit, soul, body, strength, time, talents, character, reputation, possessions, etc.—and then lay everything absolutely and unreservedly upon the altar.

If the blessing we seek is in any measure withheld, the cause will usually be a lack of whole-hearted surrender. We are holding back something that God is calling upon us to give over. In our view, perhaps, it is a very little thing, and does not matter. Yet in God's sight that little thing is the key to the whole situation.

The story is told of an Indian-famine orphan, who gave the Lord a little box that was very precious to her and in which she had kept her private trinkets. The box was shut tight and locked. However, the child could not rest, and after several hours of conflict with her own heart, she brought the key and gave it to the missionary. It had cost the little girl more to surrender the key than it had to give up the box. Beloved, in giving Christ your heart have you kept the key? I beseech you to make a clean breast of everything, for God demands of everyone "an unconditional surrender." Accept now the challenge the Lord makes in Malachi 3:10: " 'Bring the whole tithe into the storehouse, that there may be food in my house. Test me in this,' says the Lord Almighty, 'and see if I will not throw open the floodgates of heaven and pour out so much blessing that you will not have room enough for it.' "

3. It must be *final.*
Unless surrender is final, it cannot be called true

surrender. When rightly understood, surrender to God can neither be repeated nor recalled; it is unalterable and irrevocable. There are Christians who have a habit of making a reconsecration of their lives on every favorable occasion. Indeed, some believers give themselves anew to God with each recurring day. The motive that prompts to this act is of course entirely right, but the practice itself is clearly unscriptural. Thus Paul declared: "because I know whom I have believed, and am convinced that he is able to guard what I have entrusted to him for that day" (2 Timothy 1:12).

One step of surrender, therefore, if it is intelligent and involves the whole life, should be sufficient.

Nor can the step of surrender, when once taken, be recalled, for it is a definite committal of the whole life to God. Now, the act of committal implies two parties—God and the believer. Neither party without the consent of the other can alter the terms of or withdraw from the transaction. Beloved, when you lay yourself with all your interests upon the altar, God accepts your sacrifice and seals it forever. There are, indeed, only two conditions upon which your step of full surrender could be repeated or recalled. The first is that God Himself should give back what you lay upon the altar and the second is that you yourself should take it back. The former condition is impossible, for God will guard "what I have entrusted to him for that day." Moreover, Christ said:

> My sheep listen to my voice; I know them, and they follow me. I give them eternal life, and they

shall never perish; no one can snatch them out of
my hand. My Father, who has given them to me,
is greater than all; no one can snatch them out of
my Father's hand. (John 10:27–29)

But if the first condition is *impossible*, the second
condition is *improbable*. No truehearted child of God
is at all likely to take his gift deliberately from the
altar. Rather will he pray with the psalmist: "With
boughs in hand, join the festival procession/ up to the
horns of the altar" (Psalm 118:27b).

Although surrender should be made once for all, yet
its daily recognition becomes a means of grace. Instead of giving ourselves anew to God, every morning
let us say:

> Lord, I am Thine, entirely Thine,
> Purchased and saved by blood Divine;
> With full consent Thine would I be,
> And own Thy sov'reign right in me.

Indeed, many times a day let us look up into the face
of our Savior and whisper, "I am my Beloved's and
my Beloved is mine." Thus will He be delighted with
our confiding trust, and will sweetly respond, "I called
thee by My name, thou art Mine" (Isaiah 43:1b,
KJV).

II. An Act of Appropriating Faith.

The gift of the Holy Spirit is received not only by a
step of entire surrender but also by an act of ap-

propriating faith. These two conditions must go together and in this order. Surrender is yielding to God; faith is taking from God. Again, surrender is negative and passive, while faith is positive and aggressive. Moreover, just as the step of surrender must be voluntary, complete and final, so the act of faith must be definite, vital and appropriating.

In the act of faith through which we receive the Holy Spirit we must believe that God takes all that we give Him and that we take all that God gives us. On the Lord's side there will be no failure in taking; of this fact we may feel assured. He who has prompted the step of surrender will not refuse the gift that we bring. When we lay our hearts and lives unreservedly upon the altar, Christ accepts our offering and seals it eternally His. Moveover, the altar sanctifies the gift.

Nor on our part will there be failure in taking, if we remember that Christ gives Himself far more freely and unreservedly to us than we give ourselves to Him. Let us not wait for a thrill of emotion before we count God true to His word. The divine order is fact, faith, feeling. Whatever God says, we must believe just because He says it. Feeling will then follow in its time as a matter of course. According to a converted heathen child, "faith is believing a thing hard enough to act as if it was so." Therefore, when we have taken the step of surrender, let us count God faithful in meeting us and in giving us all our faith has dared to claim.

In the first place, let us believe that we are now identified with Christ in His crucifixion and resurrection. Let us count ourselves on the cross and in the grave with Christ. Let us count, moveover, that we are raised together with Christ and with Him are now seated "in heavenly places."

In the second place, let us believe that by our identification with Christ in His death and resurrection we have died unto sin and are living unto God. Let us count that the power of the flesh is broken, that the dominion of sin is destroyed, that self is dethroned from the heart and that Christ is enthroned within. Indeed, it is now our privilege to claim with Paul: "I have been crucified with Christ and I no longer live, but Christ lives in me" (Galatians 2:20a).

Abide forever

In the third place, and highest of all, let us believe that we have received the Holy Spirit and been baptized with power from on high. Let us count that by the incoming and indwelling of the Holy Spirit, Christ has been made unto us sanctification. Beloved, "the Comforter is come!" Before this He has been *with* you, but after this He will be *within* you. Nor will the Holy Spirit leave His temple which He now occupies and possesses. *He has come to abide forever.* Glory! Like Christ after His baptism, your whole life from this solemn hour will be wrought out in continual and absolute dependence upon the Spirit of God.

It is through the Holy Spirit that the Father will manifest Himself to you. It is through the Holy Spirit that Christ will reveal Himself in you. It is through the Holy Spirit that you will resist the devil in meeting and overcoming temptation. It is through the

Holy Spirit that you will live a holy life. It is through the Holy Spirit that you will triumph in suffering and rise victorious over sorrow. It is through the Holy Spirit that you will speak messages full of life and power to the sinful and needy. And it is through the Holy Spirit that you will perform deeds that will extend the kingdom of God upon earth and thus hasten the return of our Lord.

Two divine personalities

We have said that it is through the incoming and indwelling of the Holy Spirit that Christ is enthroned in our hearts and is made unto us sanctification. Here, then, are two divine Personalities. How can both Christ and the Holy Spirit dwell within us and how can we be sure that we always give to both equal recognition and honor? A little reflection will relieve these questions of perplexity. The Holy Spirit comes to us as the Spirit of Christ, baptized with His personal presence. In the Old Testament He is revealed as the Spirit of the Father, but in the New Testament He is revealed as the Spirit of the Son. Again, it is the office work of the Holy Spirit to represent Christ—to call attention to Him, to speak of Him, and to glorify Him. Thus, Jesus said:

> But when he, the Spirit of truth, comes, he will guide you into all truth. He will not speak on his own; he will speak only what he hears, and he will tell you what is yet to come. He will bring glory to me by taking from what is mine and

making it known to you. All that belongs to the
Father is mine. That is why I said the Spirit will
take from what is mine and make it known to
you. (John 16:13–15)

If it were not for our atmosphere, the sun, although
a ball of fire, would shine coldly, lie a twinkling star.
But the atmosphere, which envelopes the earth,
receives the rays of the sun and transmutes them into
color, heat and light. Likewise, if it were not for the
Holy Spirit, Christ, who is seated at the right hand of
God, could only be honored and worshiped as our
risen and ascended Lord. But the Holy Spirit, who is
the Breath of God, receives Christ and reveals Him to
our hearts as Life, Light and Truth. When we look
through a telescope, we do not see the lens but the object that the lens brings near. So when we look
through the Holy Spirit, so to speak, we behold
Christ, not seated yonder in heavenly glory but reign-
ing within on the throne of our hearts. Indeed, when
we are filled with the Spirit, we shall be conscious not
so much of the presence of the Spirit as of the person
of the Lord. Let us, therefore, occupy ourselves with
Christ, while the Spirit of Truth undrapes His radiant
figure, and standing in the background, bids us gaze
on His dear face.

Beloved, we have crossed the River Jordan. We have
passed out of the "waste, howling wilderness" and are
"over in the land of Canaan." The seventh chapter of
Romans with its ceaseless struggles and discouraging
defeats is in the past, and we are living in the eighth
chapter with its grateful rest and welcome deliverance.

The vision of victory has been transformed into a glorious reality.

Now, when a radical and revolutionary transformation like this takes place in our hearts and lives we will certainly know it. Moreover, we may expect the Holy Spirit to witness as definitely and as distinctly to His work of sanctification as He does to his work of regeneration. But while this is true, the witness in every case will not be the same either in kind or in degree. There are of course temperamental differences in people, and there are varying types of Christian experience, corresponding to these differences, which a knowledge of psychology helps us to understand and explain. For example, there are demonstrative persons. When such persons experience sanctification, the witness of the Spirit is quite likely to take the form of exalted feeling or even ecstatic emotion. On the other hand, there are dispassionate persons. In their case there is apt to be little, if any, feeling, but they will have a deep, quiet sense of spiritual satisfaction. But however this may be, the point to be emphasized is that in every instance of sanctification the witness of the Spirit, both in kind and degree, should be *satisfactory to the believer himself who is sanctified.* Moreover, a truly sanctified life will "bring forth fruit unto God" and this fruit—the fruit of the Spirit—will be manifest to all.

It is not necessary for a Christian worker to notify a sinner when he is saved. The new light on the countenance, the new song on the lips, the new spirit of prayer, the new love for God—these and many other similar evidences of conversion will be seen and known of all men. Furthermore, God has promised to give to each regenerated heart the witness of its acceptance. In like manner, it will not be necessary for a Christian worker or a fellow believer to notify a child of God when he has received the Holy Spirit and taken Christ as his sanctification. Indeed, spiritual injury has been done to many a soul by this practice. Beloved, if the Holy Spirit has come to your heart to abide forever, He will surely let you know it. Nor will He keep you long waiting. Do not be satisfied with anyone's assurances upon this point. Resolve to hear direct from heaven for yourself. Of course you must take the Holy Spirit by faith, but it is your privilege soon to have your claim of faith sealed by the certainty of personal knowledge. A failure at this point now will only mean perplexity of mind and disappointment of heart later on. Therefore, take your Bible and go alone with God. Continue to wait upon Him until you get an answer and are sure that you can say "yes" to the vitally important question that Paul asked the disciples of Ephesus: "Have ye received the Holy Spirit since ye believed?" (Acts 19:2b, KJV).

The Law of Reckoning

There are two working principles, so to speak, of Christian holiness, namely: the Law of Reckoning and the Life of Abiding. The meaning and value of these must now be unfolded.

The principle of reaction meets us in the operations of grace as well as in the forces of nature. Mountain tops of spiritual blessing are generally followed by valleys of spiritual depression. The making of the covenant with God, whereby we receive the Holy Spirit through surrender and faith, is usually accompanied by a state of exalted religious emotion. In the course of a few hours, however, the spiritual atmosphere will be entirely changed. The flood tide of religious elevation has naturally been succeeded by the ebb tide of religious depression. The heavenly outlook that only yesterday was bathed in the radiance of divine glory today wears an aspect of somber hue. The warmth, light and life of the new-found joy have gone from the heart, leaving it cold, and dark and dead.

Dear friend, have you had this experience? Is this

your experience now? Are you surrounded by an atmosphere of unreality and insincerity? In the absence of all spiritual feeling are you tempted to believe that you are playing the part of a hypocrite in claiming that you have received the Holy Spirit? Still more than this: Does the old life that you have nailed to the cross seem to come back with all its power of evil suggestion and lustful desire? In fact, do you "feel just the same as ever," and as if the glorious experience of yesterday were nothing but a fading dream?

Only a temptation

Beloved, such an experience is only a temptation, the work of Satan, to discourage your heart and destroy your faith. The devil takes advantage of the natural reaction of the soul from a season of perhaps intense spiritual exaltation to create an atmosphere of unreality and to try to make you feel insincere and even hypocritical in your honest claim of faith that you have received the Holy Spirit. Moreover, the devil has the power to bring back, in thought and feeling, the shadow of your former self. He will endeavor to make you believe that the vision of victory has not been transformed into a glorious reality.

What, then, is to be done? Why, such an experience as this is just the spiritual condition to which the law of reckoning applies. Let us, therefore, try to get a clear idea of the nature and operation of this law. Indeed, its importance cannot easily be overestimated; for when rightly understood it must be recognized as one of the fundamental principles of the new life of holiness in Christ. In Romans 6:11 Paul says "In the same way, count yourselves dead to sin but alive to God in Christ Jesus."

Now, there is a Greek word, occurring about 40 times in the New Testament, which is variously translated in the Authorized Version "reckon," "count" and "impute." Literally, it signifies to put things together. And then, to calculate or compute. In its ordinary use, reckoning is a mathematical term, and denotes a cold, calculating operation of the reasoning faculty. The process is devoid of poetic sentiment and even of sensation. Thus, when a merchant makes out his accounts or balances his books, the operation is one of pure computation, and the result is *reckoned* according to the fixed laws of numbers.

Spiritually, reckoning is simply counting that to be true which the Bible declares to be true. It is our amen to what God says. Thus the New Testament states that by our union with Christ in His death and resurrection we are "dead indeed unto sin, but alive unto God." Apart from all feeling, therefore, we count this to be true; and as we boldly maintain this attitude, God transforms "faith reckonings into glorious realities."

Thus, reckoning is the key to a victorious Christian life. Indeed, it is the pole star of the believer's walk with God. In this state of depression for example, when the spiritual atmosphere is charged with a sense of insincerity and unreality, we must maintain our attitude of victory by the law of reckoning. We must count that God makes real *in* us by the Spirit all that Christ has made *for* us on the cross. We must steadfastly *reckon* that we are dead unto sin and alive unto God. We must steadfastly reckon that we have received the Holy Spirit. We must steadfastly reckon that Christ has been made unto us sanctification. There are, indeed, some people who seem to make light of reckoning, calling it all a "make believe." But surely, they cannot have fully grasped the inner spirit of the divine principle. A thing does not become true, simply because we reckon it to be true. It is just the other way. The thing is true, whether we reckon it to be true or not. But our act of reckoning does make it experimentally real. And moreover, while there is no sentiment or emotion in the law of reckoning, there is a good deal of both sentiment and emotion in the practical victory that the operation of the law brings.

Now, it is of the utmost importance that we clearly understand just what it is that we are to reckon. We are to reckon that *we ourselves are "in the same way . . . dead to sin but alive to God in Christ Jesus"* (Romans 6:11). This expression requires the most careful consideration.

First, dead to sin

In the first place, we are to reckon ourselves *dead to sin*. Sin is not dead, but we are dead to sin. There is a vast difference between these two things. What, then, does it mean to be dead to sin? According to the scientist, life is "the correspondence of an inner organism with its outer environment." When this "correspondence" ceases the result is death. Following out this explanation, we may say that a person is "dead" to a thing, when he is out of "correspondence" with that thing. Thus, a blind man is dead to light and color. Light and color exist, but not for him; he has no eyes with which to behold the faces of loved ones, or to enjoy the beauties of nature. Again, the deaf man is dead to sound. Sound exists, but not for him; he has no ears with which to hear the voices of friends or be charmed by the harmonies of music. Now, in like manner are we dead to sin. By nature we are in correspondence with sin; but by union with Christ in His death and resurrection and by the incoming and indwelling of the Holy Spirit we are out of correspondence with it. Sin exists, but not for us. While we abide in Christ and walk in the Spirit we are dead alike to its presence and power.

Preoccupation of mind

Another illustration is preoccupation of mind. Some people have such intense power of mental concentration as for the time being to become entirely preoccupied with the thing in hand. They will pass a friend on the street without salutation or even recognition. When spoken to, they will not answer. Indeed, something extraordinary must occur in order to divert their mind or arrest their attention. For the time being they are "dead" to their surroundings. So by our preoccupation with Christ and with the things of the Spirit we become dead to sin. The world, the flesh and the devil with their seductive temptations are all around us, but while we abide in Christ and walk in the Spirit we are insulated from their destructive power.

Second, alive to God

In the second place, we are to reckon ourselves *alive to God.* "Dead to sin" is the negative side of our reckoning; "alive to God" is the positive side. Now, the sinner is out of correspondence with God. He is "dead in trespasses and sins."

The Christian, however, is in correspondence with God. He walks "in newness of life." The believer is "alive to God." Indeed, the deeper walk of the Holy Spirit in sanctification quickens every spiritual sense. By the heavenly anointing our eyes are opened to see divine truth; our ears are unstopped to hear "the still, small voice"; our taste is renewed to feed upon the "living bread"; our touch is refined to detect the presence of Christ; and we become of "quick understanding in the fear of the Lord" (Isaiah 11:3, KJV). Moreover, by the incoming of the Spirit and the indwelling of Christ our whole being is made "alive to God." There is a quickening of every faculty and power of the mind and every member and organ of the body.

Third, through Jesus Christ our Lord

But in the third place, we are to reckon ourselves dead to sin, and alive to God *through Jesus Christ our Lord.* In ourselves we are not dead to sin nor alive to God. It is Christ Himself who puts us out of correspondence with sin and puts us in correspondence with God. If our reckoning is to be made real, we must, therefore,

abide in Christ and walk in the Spirit. As our union
with the Lord was established by an act of appropriating faith so it must be maintained by an attitude of
steadfast reckoning.

Let us clearly understand, then, that the devil has
power to bring back the shadow of the old life, but
that we must meet his attack by the reckoning of
faith. We must learn that Satan can insinuate evil sug-
gestions into our minds and project sinful desires into
our hearts. It is his device to manufacture and over-
shadow us with a personality closely resembling our
former self and then try to palm off as ours this work
of his own invention. Indeed, it is at this point that
many Christians who have entered the deeper life fail
because of ignorance and lack of reckoning. When the
"old man" that has been nailed to the cross comes
back in wicked thoughts and carnal desires, they do
not recognize the trick of the enemy, which they
should repudiate and ignore. Partly in fear because of
the experience, and partly in discouragement because
of the temptation, they are led to identify themselves
with their dead and buried past, and thus they fall an
easy prey to its ensnaring influence and destructive
power. A corpse must be kept under ground, or it will
cause death to the living. So the "old man" must be
kept by faith in the grave of Christ, or he will pollute
our hearts and minds and destroy our faith.

Thus, the law of reckoning is the secret of victory. A
bold claim of faith will save us from being engulfed by
the waves of reaction and keep us from discouragement and despair in the hour of depression. Remember, beloved, that the thing that seems real is the

unreal and the thing that seems unreal is real. The insincerity and unreality that envelope you like the atmosphere, are only apparent. It is the work of Satan.

The vision of victory *is* a glorious reality. The Comforter *has* come. Christ *now* reigns within on the throne of your heart. Hallelujah! Between you and the "old man" stands forever the cross of Christ. The self-life that would again fasten itself upon you is no longer yours. Never can the past come back for it is buried forever in the grave of Christ. Therefore, no matter what the devil says, refuse to believe it. Discount your feelings, whatever they may be. In spite of everything reckon that God meets your trust and that the victory is yours. Ignore, then, the shadow of the past which Satan brings back. Do not fear it. Fear will paralyze your faith and make you an easy prey to sin. Repudiate the shadow as something from which you have been separated and are henceforth forever detached. If you will treat the shadow thus, it will vanish like the mist before the morning sun. It will disappear like a specter of the night.

> Let us reckon, reckon, reckon,
>   Let us reckon, rather feel;
> Let us be true to the reck'ning,
>   And He will make it real.

The Life of Abiding

On our part contact with God is maintained not only by the law of reckoning but also by the life of abiding. Holiness flows from union with Christ, and apart from abiding in Him we have no purity or fruitfulness. Thus Jesus said:

> Remain in me, and I will remain in you. No branch can bear fruit by itself; it must remain in the vine. Neither can you bear fruit unless you remain in me.
>
> I am the vine; you are the branches. If a man remains in me and I in him, he will bear much fruit; apart from me you can do nothing. (John 15:4–5)

Abide is a familiar but interesting word. The Greek verb is *meno* or *menein*, from which comes the English word *remain*, and which is rendered in the Authorized Version by a number of expressions, for example: abide, dwell, remain, continue, tarry, endure, be present, etc. With reference to our union with Christ a good translation would be *live*. Thus in John 15:9, "*remain* in My love," the force of Christ's command would be better brought out by reading, "*live* in My love."

To abide in Christ means two things, namely: *obedience* and *fellowship*. By keeping the commandments of God and abiding with Him through the Spirit we abide in Christ.

I. Obedience.

In 1 John 3:24, abiding in Christ is described as a life of obedience: "Those who obey his commands live in him, and he in them. And this is how we know that he lives in us: We know it by the Spirit he gave us."

One of the ringing messages of the Old Testament is the absolute necessity of perfect obedience. Thus, the high estimate that God placed upon the observance of His law is seen in the solemn words of Samuel the prophet to Saul the rejected king:

> Does the Lord delight in burnt offerings and
> sacrifices
>   as much as in obeying the voice of the Lord?
> To obey is better than sacrifice,
>   and to heed is better than the fat of rams.
> For rebellion is like the sin of divination,
>   and arrogance like the evil of idolatry.
> Because you have rejected the word of the Lord,
>   he has rejected you as king.
>   (1 Samuel 15:22–23)

But Israel did not keep the law nor obey the voice of the Lord. Yet the cause was not in the law, which was "holy, just and good," but in the people who were weak, wayward and wicked. In the midst of the national failure, however, the prophets foretold a time when the law of God would be obeyed and when His voice would be obeyed:

> "This is the covenant I will make with the house
>   of Israel
>   after that time," declares the Lord.
> "I will put my law in their minds
>   and write it on their hearts.
> I will be their God,
>   and they will be my people." (Jeremiah 31:33)

I will give them an undivided heart and put a new spirit in them; I will remove from them their heart of stone and give them a heart of flesh. Then they will follow my decrees and be careful to keep my laws. They will be my people, and I will be their God. (Ezekiel 11:19–20)

I will sprinkle clean water on you, and you will be clean; I will cleanse you from all your impurities and from all your idols. I will give you a new heart and put a new spirit in you; I will remove from you your heart of stone and give you a heart of flesh. And I will put my Spirit in you and move you to follow my decrees and be careful to keep my laws. (Ezekiel 36:25–27)

Literally, these glorious promises must be referred to Israel, but spiritually they may be applied to the Church. For the Church they were fulfilled at Pentecost, and are for believers to claim in the present age.

Even more strongly, if possible, than the Old Testament does the New Testament emphasize the absolute necessity of perfect obedience. Thus, in His parting address to His disciples Jesus said:

> If you love me, you will obey what I command.
>
> Whoever has my commands and obeys them, he is the one who loves me. He who loves me will be loved by my Father, and I too will love him and show myself to him.
>
> If anyone loves me, he will obey my teaching. My Father will love him, and we will come to him and make our home with him. He who does not love me will not obey my teaching. The words you hear are not my own; they belong to the Father who sent me. (John 14:15, 21, 23–24)
>
> If you remain in me and my words remain in you, ask whatever you wish, and it will be given you.
>
> If you obey my commands, you will remain in my love, just as I have obeyed my Father's commands and remain in his love. (John 15:7, 10)

Now, although Israel could not obey the law of God, yet Christians can keep the commandments of

Christ. Indeed, Jesus made obedience an essential mark of true discipleship. "You are my friends, if you do what I command" (John 15:14).

In Ezekiel 36:27 we read: "And I will put my Spirit in you and move you to follow my decrees and be careful to keep my laws."

Here the prophet declares that the incoming of the Holy Ghost will have a causative power unto obedience. As a result of the Spirit's indwelling, the promise is, not that we *may* but that we *will* obey the voice of the Lord and walk in His holy ways. Again, in Romans 8:3–4, we read:

> For what the law was powerless to do in that it was weakened by the sinful nature, God did by sending his own Son in the likeness of sinful man to be a sin offering. And so he condemned sin in sinful man, in order that the righteous requirements of the law might be fully met in us, who did not live according to the sinful nature but according to the Spirit.

Here the apostle declares that the purpose of the incarnation of Christ and the incoming of the Spirit is "that the righteous requirements of the law might be fully met in us, who did not live according to the sinful nature but according to the Spirit." In other words, the sanctifying work of the Holy Spirit in our lives will be to produce that renewal of character and righteousness of conduct that the law fails to produce.

Christians today do no have to try to keep the commandments of Christ in the same way that Israel of old tried to keep the commandments of God, and utterly failed. For, in their efforts to observe the law of Moses and obey the voice of the Lord the chosen people struggled hopelessly against an evil heart and a perverse will. To believers, however, has been given a changed heart and in their inmost parts has been written the divine law. Thus, obedience is the product of holiness—the fruit of the incoming of the Spirit and the indwelling of Christ.

In a popular manual on the deeper life the writer tells of a willful and wayward boy, whose mother had, without avail, tried every means within her power to make teachable and obedient. One day in despair, she said to a sympathetic friend: "I wish I could get inside my boy, and think through his mind, and love through his heart, and act through his will. If I could only do this, I would soon make him teachable and obedient, for I would cause him to think pure thoughts, and love good things, and always do what is right."

Beloved, the futile wish of the fond mother for her boy, is gloriously realized by God in the lives of His children. Though we often desire to do right, yet in ourselves we are weak and wayward, with a rebellious will and a disobedient heart. In our own strength we cannot keep the commandments of Christ, nor fulfill the perfect will of God. But Christ Himself by the Holy Spirit will come and live within us. To us He will give the hearkening ear to hear "the still, small voice," and the yielded heart to "walk in the Spirit." Then we will be enabled to keep His commandments and please the Father in all things. Thus, through our hearts will pulsate His holy desires, and through our wills His sublime purposes will be wrought out. May we not pray:

> Live out Thy life in me,
>   Live out Thy life in me;
> By Thy wonderful power,
>   By Thy grace every hour,
> Live out Thy life in me.

II. Fellowship.

In John 6:56–57, abiding in Christ is described as a life of communion or fellowship: "Whoever eats my flesh and drinks my blood remains in me, and I in him. Just as the living Father sent me and I live because of the Father, so the one who feeds on me will live because of me."

Fellowship is an attractive and suggestive term. The Greek noun, *koinonia,* literally signifies partnership or participation. The word is used to express the intimacy, communion and oneness that exist between Christ and the believer.

> But he who unites himself with the Lord is one with him in spirit. (1 Corinthians 6:17)

> And our fellowship is with the Father and with his Son, Jesus Christ.
>   But if we walk in the light, as he is in the light, we have fellowship with one another, and the

blood of Jesus, his Son, purifies us from all sin. (1 John 1:3b, 7)

Our Lord's chosen symbol of the union and communion of the believer with Himself was the vine and the branches. Now, the relationship between obedience and fellowship may be illustrated by the connection between the grapes and the sap. Grapes are the fruit of sap, while sap is the source of grapes. Each is related to the other, while both in turn are dependent upon the vine. So obedience is the fruit of fellowship, while fellowship is the spring of obedience. Each is related to the other, while both in turn are dependent upon Christ. In fact, without true fellowship there can be no practical obedience. And without practical obedience there can be no true fellowship.

Glorious, however, as is the reception of the Holy Spirit, it is not the climax of spiritual life. It is only a unique crisis, which marks a new beginning in Christian experience. After the *baptism* comes the *fullness* of the Spirit. After the bond of union with Christ has been established the life of communion with Him must be maintained. Indeed, in the blessed experience of sanctification we will never be able to comprehend, much less to compass, all the heights and depths the lengths and breadths, of the matchless love and infinite power of God. In First Corinthians 12:13, we read: "For we were all baptized by one Spirit into one body—whether Jews or Greeks, slave or free—and we were all given the one Spirit to drink."

Again in Ephesians 5:18b, Paul exhorts believers: "Be filled with the Spirit" (literally, in the Spirit).

Now, the fullness of the Spirit marks an advance upon the baptism of the Spirit. The divine gift of the Spirit, like the new birth by the Spirit, is as we have seen, a distinct act and a definite transaction. There is a time when we take Christ to be our Savior, and there is a moment when we take Him to be our Sanctifier through the incoming of the Holy Spirit. The fullness of the Spirit, however, is quite different from these experiences. Unlike them it is not an act, but a process. It is not a transaction, but a habit. Having received Christ (act), we grow up into Him in all things (process). Having received the Holy Spirit (transaction), we drink, and keep drinking of His fullness (habit). Thus, the infilling of the Spirit is the life of fellowship with Christ.

But this is just the point where many earnest children of God who are seeking the fullness of divine blessing fail of the complete satisfaction of every need of spirit, mind and body. They have received the Holy Spirit; this they dare not doubt. Moreover, they have had what to others as well as to themselves is clear and convincing evidence that "the Comforter has come." Yet their lives are without rest and joy, without power and fruit. Indeed, their hearts are "one vast continent of unexplored longings and unsatisfied desires."

Beloved, is this your experience? Have you been wondering what the trouble is? Let me tell you. You have taken Christ to be your Sanctifier, but you have not "followed on to know the Lord." You are not living in His love. You have received the Holy Spirit as your Abiding Comforter, but you have not been drinking in His joy and power. You are not "filled with the Spirit."

What do you think would happen to a diver who, when under the water, does not breathe through his air tube? Dear friend, you are spiritually starving. Your life is like a bottle corked tight in the ocean. All around is the limitless sea, yet the bottle inside is empty and dry. Spiritually open up your whole being to God. Wait upon the Lord. Study the Word. Feed upon Christ. Drink in the peace and rest, the joy and power of the Holy Spirit. Learn to live by the moment every time you feel spiritual hunger, feed upon the Living Bread. Every time you feel spiritual thirst, drink of the Living Water. Thus will you know the joys of fellowship with Christ, and your whole life will be kept fresh, fragrant and fruitful in the fullness of the Spirit.

The Broken Circuit

It cannot be too strongly emphasized that holiness is retained only while vital contact with Christ is maintained. On our side this divine contact may be interrupted and even temporarlily broken. Now, an interrupted or broken circuit, when it occurs, always results in a darkening of the spiritual sky, a loss of conscious fellowship with Chirst and a lack of real victory in the life. This experience may be illustrated from electricity. In order to make a circuit the wires from the positive and negative poles of a battery must be brought together. This forms the contact; and the electric current depends on the contact. Breaking the contact interrupts or destroys the current. The separation of the wires need not be great—only just so that they do not touch. In like manner, our holiness depends upon contact with God. Anything that breaks or impairs this vital contact, however slight it may be, interrupts our communion with Christ and brings defeat instead of victory into our lives.

Now, there is just one thing and one thing only that

can cause an interrupted or broken circuit between the soul and Chirst. This is sin. *Sin breaks the contact.* But let it be clearly understood that when we say that sin breaks the contact, we refer not to the practice or habit of sin, but to the commission of a single or solitary act of sin. It is true that regeneration destroys the *love* of sin and that sanctification breaks the *power* of sin. No one who has been truly converted and received the Holy Spirit can possibly thereafter live in sin or habitually practice sin. This is the clear teaching of First John 3:6, 9:

> No one who lives in him keeps on sinning. No one who continues to sin has either seen him or known him.
> No one who is born of God will continue to sin, because God's seed remains in him; he cannot go on sinning, because he has been born of God.

In these passages the italicized verbs are in the present tense, which in Greek denotes *continuous or repeated action.* In each instance the expression "practice sin" will better bring out the force of the original. Thus we may render as follows: "No one who lives in him practices sin. No one who continues to practice sin has either seen him or known him." Again: "No one who is born of God will practice sin, because God's seed remains in him; he cannot practice sin, because he has been born of God." See also Galatians 5:21, where the Greek verb is translated "practice" in the Revised Version.

But while this is all gloriously true, it is not true that a believer can ever reach a state of grace, where *it is not possible to commit an act of sin*. In Galatians 6:1, Paul says:

> Brothers, if someone is caught in a *sin* (literally the word means *a falling aside*), you who are spiritual should restore him gently. But watch yourself, or you also may be tempted.

Moreover, in First John 2:1, the apostle says:

> My dear children, I write this to you so *that you will not sin*. But if anybody does *sin*, we have one who speaks to the Father in our defense—Jesus Christ, the Righteous One.

Here the italicized verbs are not in the present tense but in the aorist tense, which denotes a single and solitary act. Yet even such an experience is not necessary, for the apostle distinctly states: "I write these things to you so *that you will not sin*"—that is, that you may not commit even an act of sin. Indeed Jude declares that God is "able to keep you from falling (R.V. stumbling), and to present you before his glorious presence without fault and with great joy" (verse 24).

The sin that interrupts or breaks the believer's contact with Christ may be occasioned in various ways. It may, for example, be due to a failure in reckoning. Because of fear of the shadow of the past or because of the pressure of temptation you may have taken your eyes from Christ and fallen under the power of the old life. Again, it may be due to unsteadfastness in abiding. The secret of abiding is not mastered in a moment; and you may have stumbled or fallen in honest but mistaken efforts to keep Christ's commandments and live in His love. Still again, it may have resulted from disobedience to "the still, small voice." Perhaps you have not met God squarely in some of His dealings with you. You have not kept saying yes to Christ. You have not been careful in little things always to "walk in the Spirit." You yourself, dear friend, know just what happened; or, if you do not know and will be honest with God, He will show you. At any rate your contact with God has in some way been broken. You are not enjoying conscious fellowship with Christ. Your spiritual sky is overcast with clouds. You are not in victory. And the reason is: *You have sinned.*

Two grave perils

Two grave perils should be avoided because they move a soul out of fellowship with Christ. One is the temptation to discouragement and despair. The other is the unwillingness to acknowledge sin and even the attempt to evade and ignore it.

On the one hand, discouragement and despair, which are always the work of the enemy, expose the soul to fierce temptations and make it an easy prey to presumptuous sins. Consequently, if you have a fall, beloved, do not allow yourself to become discouraged nor plunged in despair. The fall is indeed sad, but it is not hopeless. There is of course a prestige that comes from never losing a battle; but the loss of a battle does not necessarily involved the loss of a campaign. Many a campaign has been lost, yet a war has been won. Be encouraged! Remember that on God's side the contact is not broken. He still holds you safe in His almighty arms. Moreover, nothing can separate you from the love of Christ. And the blessed Comforter has promised to abide with you forever. But for a moment the Lord is in hiding. Because of your sin a cloud has come between you and your Savior. As of old you cannot see His blessed face nor feel the thrill of His radiant presence.

On the other hand, the unwillingness to acknowledge sin and the attempt either to evade or ignore it is even a graver peril than the temptation to discouragement and despair. Such a dangerous attitude toward sin is the result either of the deceptive snare of Satan or of unscriptural views of sanctification. It is one of the devices of the devil to try to blind us to the "exceeding sinfulness of sin."

Again, those who believe in "sinless perfection" can never of course consistently admit that they can commit sin. To them there must be some other explanation. So, what the Scriptures call sin, they call "an error of judgment," "an innocent mistake," "an infirmity of tempter," "righteous indignation" or some other equally mild and delusive term. An act cannot be wrong, they contend, if the motive that prompts it is right. Thus, not having in their view, committed sin, they have no confession of sin to make. My beloved friend, beware of such trifling with sin. It will so dull your moral sense that soon you will not be able to discriminate between right and wrong. Sin is a horrible monster! Unless confessed and pardoned, it will separate the soul from God. For a time indeed you may have a fancied feeling of security, but in the end your faith will be destroyed and you yourself plunged into the darkness of hopeless ruin and utter despair.

The only remedy

Now, there is one and only one remedy for sin. This is the blood of Christ. Consequently, there is one and but one way in which an interrupted or broken contact with Christ can be restored, and this is by the honest confession of sin and its complete cleansing by the blood. Beloved, whenever you feel yourself out of conscious touch with Christ, go at once to the blood. Do not lose a moment. Delay is perilous. Do not attempt to justify yourself or indulge in vain regrets. Confess your sin to God at once and seek full pardon and complete cleansing. Keep nothing back; make a clean breast of everything. Call sin by its right name. For example, if you have manifested impatience or irritability of temper, if you have given way to anger, jealousy or any other form of passion, do not call it nervousness or peculiarity of temperment. Own up squarely that it is *sin*. Moreover, if you have wronged a brother or sister in Christ, apologize—make complete reparation and, if necessary, full restitution before you seek pardon and cleansing from God.

If in this way you will meet God in honest confession, He will meet you in complete cleansing. His promise is this: "If we confess our sins, he is faithful and just and will forgive us our sins and purify us from all unrighteousness" (1 John 1:9).

Thus will the Lord lift the burden of condemnation, dispel the overhanging clouds of darkness, bring you back into conscious fellowship with Himself, and restore to you "the joys of His salvation." But do not wait for feeling. Take God at His word. Believe that He meets you in complete cleansing and in full restoration. Then at once resume your former attitude of reckoning and take your old place of fellowship, thus learning by your humbling experience to listen to the still, small voice and to walk in the Spirit, and trusting the Lord more fully than ever to "keep you from falling and to present you before his glorious presence without fault and with great joy—to the only God our Savior be glory, majesty, power and authority, through Jesus Christ our Lord, before all ages, now and forevermore! Amen" (Jude 24–25).

The Uplook and the Outlook

To a holy life there is both an uplook and an outlook. The uplook is the blessed hope of Christ's return. We must be holy to meet the Lord in the air and to receive the reward which His coming will bring. The outlook is the worldwide harvest field. We are saved to serve. We are sanctified to minister the riches of divine grace to the sinful and needy.

The Uplook

To a holy heart is granted a heavenly vision. Eyes that are cleared of the mists of sin behold undimmed the face of the Lord. Thus Jesus said: "Blessed are the pure in heart,/ for they will see God" (Matthew 5:8). Again, the writer of the epistle to the Hebrews says: "Make every effort to live in peace with all men and to be holy; without holiness no one will see the Lord" (12:14).

Now, the personal return of our blessed Lord is the highest incentive to a holy life. In First John we read:

How great is the love the Father has lavished on us, that we should be called children of God! And that is what we are! The reason the world does not know us is that it did not know him. Dear friends, now we are children of God, and what we will be has not yet been made known. But we know that when he appears, we shall be like him, for we shall see him as he is. Everyone who has this hope in him purifies himself, just as he is pure. (3:1–3)

Among the children of God there is a growing belief that the return of Christ is near at hand. The exact time of His coming, however, is uncertain. Nevertheless, it is our duty to watch for the appearing of Christ, and be ready to meet Him, when He comes in the air.

The story is told of a father, who once went on a journey, leaving word with his family that he expected to return by a certain train on an appointed day. When the day arrived, the mother washed and dressed the children and sent them to the depot to meet their father. But he did not come. So the following day the children went again, and the next day after, and still the next. Indeed, they continued every day to meet that train, until at last the father came. One good effect of the father's uncertain arrival was that the children kept clean.

Beloved, are we keeping our hearts and lives clean in daily expectation of the return of our Lord? Some day we shall all have to meet Christ face to face. And the momentous question is: How will we meet Him? Will it be in servile fear or in childlike confidence? The beloved apostle exhorts us: "And, now, dear children, continue in him, so that when he appears we may be confident and unashamed before him at his coming" (1 John 2:28).

To this end let us heed the solemn warning of the Savior: "Therefore keep watch because you do not know when the owner of the house will come back— whether in the evening, or at midnight, or when the rooster crows, or at dawn. If he comes suddenly, do not let him find you sleeping. What I say to you, I say to everyone: 'Watch!' " (Mark 13:35–37).

To those who are slothful and unprepared Christ will appear as a righteous Judge. But to those who are watchful and prepared He will appear as a beloved Friend. But the personal return of our blessed Lord is also the truest inspiration of a holy life. In Second Peter 3:10–14, we read:

> But the day of the Lord will come like a thief. The heavens will disapppear with a roar; the elements will be destroyed by fire, and the earth and everything in it will be laid bare.
>
> Since everything will be destroyed in this way, what kind of people ought you to be? You ought to live holy and godly lives as you look forward to the day of God and speed its coming. That day will bring about the destruction of the heavens by fire, and the elements will melt in the heat. But in keeping with his promise we are looking forward to a new heaven and a new earth, the home of righteousness.

> So then, dear friends, since you are looking
> forward to this, make every effort to be found
> spotless, blameless and at peace with him.

This is an impressive example of a class of New Testament passages that represent the personal return of
Christ as the only hope of the world and the Church.
Morally, the world of today is wabbling in its orbit,
madly plunging toward despair and destruction.
Spiritually, the professing Church of this age, in the
judgment of a writer of exceptional spiritual discerne-
ment and wide observation, is in a state of petrifaction
and putrifaction—hardness and rottenness.

The only hope

The alert believer, who accurately reads "the signs of
the times," finds little encouragement to look for im-
provement. Indeed, the only hope of both the Church
and the world is the purifying fire of the day of the
Lord. According to prophecy this dispensation will
end in dissolution and destruction; but out of the
universal wreck "in keeping with his promise we are
looking forward to a new heaven and a new earth, the
home of righteousness." This millennial age of
righteousness and peace will be ushered in by the personal return of Christ. Our hope, therefore, is not in
the fading present, but in the radiant future. Indeed,
the only thing worth living for is the coming of the
Lord.

Some years ago there lived a lad in one of the states
of the Central West. Thoughtful and studious by na-

ture, yet his view of life was, of course, bounded by the mind of a boy. He loved the games and gatherings of childhood. Indeed, the anticipation of going to a birthday surprise party would give him pleasure for many a day. But the lad grew and his outlook upon life widened. Early he caught a vision of college, and he thought that to be a freshman in the great university would fill his cup of joy to the brim. In course of time the youth entered college, but found that the delights of freshman life were not all he had dreamed. Then he thought that the height of ambition must be to be a senior and graduate with honor on Commencement Day. In due time he became a senior, and in cap and gown received his degree with honor amid the plaudits of fond parents and admiring friends. But the young graduate's cup of joy was not full, and so again he widened the horizon of his ambition.

He then decided that the supreme goal of his life would be reached, if he should go through a theological seminary, become pastor of a church, and be ordained to the ministry. All this came in its time, and along with it additional academic honors and degrees. When at last, however, the young minister stood in his own pulpit, and faced his own people, he again found that his dream was unfulfilled. He realized that his heart was not satisfied. Yet he was indeed devoutly grateful that God had "counted him faithful, putting him into the ministry." Moreover, he did esteem it the most exalted privilege to preach the unsearchable riches of Christ. But he had not found the supreme goal, the true source of the highest inspiration and the deepest satisfaction of Christian life and service.

The thought came to him of attempting to build up a big church, of striving to become a great preacher, or of seeking to win distinction in scholarship. But none of these things were lofty and enduring enough to fire his mind and stir his heart to its profoundest depths. In fact, he had no ideal which completely satisfied his ambitions and which was thus worth living for. Finally, one day there came to the young minister the heavenly uplook. His faith caught the sublime vision of the glorious hope of Christ's return. His heart was filled with expectant joy. At last his early dream was fully realized. At last he had his ideal. At last he had found the supreme goal of Christian service, and the true source of the highest inspiration and the deepest satisfaction of a holy life. Since that memorable day he has taken as his glowing watchword: "Unto the coming of the Lord."

What is your ideal? What are you living for? God declares that He has set eternity in our hearts. How, then, can we ever be satisfied with the pleasures and pursuits of time? May you speedily learn that there is nothing in this world worth living for. May God give you the heavenly uplook. May your faith catch the glorious vision of Christ's return. May you, like the young minister, find "that blessed hope" to be the supreme goal of Christian service and the true source of the highest inspiration and the deepest satisfaction of a holy heart. Indeed, over your whole life may you inscribe the sublime watchword: "Look forward to the day of God and speed its coming."

The Outlook

Finally and briefly, to a holy heart there comes an outward calling. Eyes that have caught the heavenly vision are open to the harvest fields of the world. In John 4:35, Christ says: "Do you not say, 'Four months more and then the harvest'? I tell you, open your eyes and look at the fields! They are ripe for harvest."

Now, holiness means *separation for service*. The separation is unto God, but the service is for man. Yet all service for man is of course, also service for God. Therefore, sanctification, while a blessed experience, is not an end in itself; it is rather a glorious means to a still more glorious end. This end is a life of fruitful and abiding service alike to God and man. Indeed, we are saved to serve. We are sanctified to minister the riches of divine grace to the sinful and needy.

A holy heart, then, will be an unselfish heart. It will not live for itself, but will expend its consecrated energies in ready service and in willing sacrifice for others. Again, a holy heart will bear fruit unto God. Fruit is the result of the incoming of the Spirit and the indwelling of Christ. It manifests itself not only in active ministry but also in passive suffering. It includes graces of character as well as records of achievement. Finally, a holy heart will burn with missionary fire. It will have a passion for souls. It will love the lost and seek to win them. Moreover, it will be pressed in spirit toward the regions beyond.

Have you received the Holy Spirit? Have you taken

Christ to be your sanctification? Have you had a vision of the world's need? Has there come to you the outward calling? If so, then you are living an unselfish life. Then you are bringing forth fruit unto God. Then you are burning with missionary zeal. If so, then you have a passion for souls. Then you love the lost and are seeking to save them. Then you are pressed in spirit toward the regions beyond. Surely, you will go, *if* you can. Surely, you will give *what* you can. Surely, you will pray *all* you can.

> Then I heard the voice of the Lord saying, "Whom shall I send? And who will go for us?" And I said, "Here am I. Send me!" (Isaiah 6:8)

> On the first day of every week, each one of you should set aside a sum of money in keeping with his income. (1 Corinthians 16:2a)

> He told them, "The harvest is plentiful, but the workers are few. Ask the Lord of the harvest, therefore, to send out workers into his harvest field." (Luke 10:2)